D-DAY FLEET 1944,
AMERICAN SECTOR

The US Navy's Western Task Force

Brian Lane Herder
Illustrated by Edouard A. Groult

OSPREY PUBLISHING
Bloomsbury Publishing Plc
Kemp House, Chawley Park, Cumnor Hill, Oxford OX2 9PH, UK
29 Earlsfort Terrace, Dublin 2, Ireland
1385 Broadway, 5th Floor, New York, NY 10018, USA
E-mail: info@ospreypublishing.com
www.ospreypublishing.com

OSPREY is a trademark of Osprey Publishing Ltd

First published in Great Britain in 2024

A catalog record for this book is available from the British Library.

ISBN: PB 9781472863621; eBook 9781472863638; ePDF 9781472863607; XML 9781472863614

24 25 26 27 28 10 9 8 7 6 5 4 3 2 1

Maps by bounford.com
Diagrams by Adam Tooby
Index by Fionbar Lyons
Typeset by PDQ
Printed by Repro India Ltd.

Front Cover: Art by Edouard A. Groult, © Osprey Publishing
Osprey Publishing supports the Woodland Trust, the UK's leading woodland conservation charity.

To find out more about our authors and books visit www.ospreypublishing.com. Here you will find
extracts, author interviews, details of forthcoming events and the option to sign up for our newsletter.

Author's Note:
All times given are British "double summer time" unless otherwise noted.

CONTENTS

THE FLEET'S PURPOSE

"More than one fine general who had dreamed of subjugating Britain in the past had achieved only frustration through failure to propitiate the God of the Sea. … Now, the attempt was to be reversed, against a fortressed Europe lying in the chains of the Nazis."

- Rear Admiral Morton L. Deyo (USN), commander Utah Bombardment Group, June 6, 1944

USS LCT-514 seen underway conducting training exercises off Camp Bradford, Virginia, in 1943 or 1944. Although this LCT deployed to the Pacific and did not serve off Normandy, it gives an excellent profile view of what its many sisters would have looked like headed towards the French shoreline. (80-G-K-13873)

Operation *Overlord* was the June 1944 Anglo–American invasion to liberate Nazi-occupied Europe; *Overlord*'s cross-Channel assault phase against the Normandy coast was codenamed Operation *Neptune*. The formal mission of Operation *Neptune* was "to secure a lodgment on the Continent from which further offensive operations can be developed."

This title analyzes Rear Admiral Alan G. Kirk's Western Naval Task Force (WNTF), the US-commanded invasion fleet responsible for the American landings in western Normandy. Kirk deployed in the Mediterranean in 1942–43

and served as an amphibious commander for the 1943 invasions of Sicily and Italy. He was named the senior US naval commander for the *Neptune* assault and given command of the Western Naval Task Force, which he exercised from heavy cruiser USS *Augusta*. The WNTF was an operational formation under the administration of the US Twelfth Fleet, the US Navy (USN) command assigned to the United Kingdom. The WNTF was accordingly designated Task Force 122, with its constituent forces likewise receiving designations beginning with "12."

Kirk's mission was to successfully land and reinforce the vanguard units of Lieutenant-General Omar Bradley's First US Army on the western Normandy beaches. Immediately to the east, a simultaneous British landing would carve out its own Normandy beachhead. Together, the Anglo-Americans intended their initial Normandy lodgment to grow into a theaterwide ground offensive that would ultimately drive into Germany and force the Nazi regime's unconditional surrender.

The US landing zone at Normandy was divided into two sectors, codenamed "Utah" and "Omaha." Kirk's WNTF was likewise subdivided into two assault forces corresponding to each sector. The Utah assault force (Task Force 125, or TF 125) was commanded by Rear Admiral Don P. Moon, while the Omaha assault force (TF 124) was commanded by Rear Admiral John L. Hall. In addition to 16,000 paratroopers, the Americans expected to put 57,000 combat troops ashore on D-Day, with 23,000 at Utah and 34,000 at Omaha. This made Omaha the largest single landing force on D-Day, exceeding the 29,000-strong Sword landings in the British zone. The two American sectors would ultimately produce the lightest ground casualties of the entire Normandy assault (Utah) as well as the heaviest (Omaha).

A SHAEF staff conference from January 2, 1944. From left to right: Lieutenant-General Omar Bradley, Admiral Sir Bertram Ramsay, Air Chief Marshal Sir Arthur Tedder, General Dwight D. Eisenhower, General Sir Bernard Montgomery, Air Chief Marshal Sir Trafford Leigh-Mallory, and Lieutenant-General Walter Bedell Smith. (Public Domain)

FLEET FIGHTING POWER

THE SHIPS

The USN commanded the WNTF and provided most combat power and heavy lift capacity. However, the WNTF also comprised warships, auxiliaries, and even entire flotillas from many different nations and service branches.

The USN was not even the only American seagoing branch off western Normandy. The United States Coast Guard (USCG) manned roughly 70 ships, including numerous LSTs (Landing Ship, Tanks), LCI(L)s, (Landing Craft, Infantry), and a rescue flotilla of thirty 83ft USCG cutters. The USCG additionally crewed the ostensibly USN transports USS *Barnett*, *Charles Carroll*, *Joseph T. Dickman*, and *Samuel Chase*, along with the transports' associated landing craft. A USCG captain even commanded an entire Utah assault group.

Britain's Royal Navy made the second-largest national contribution to the WNTF, including one monitor, one heavy cruiser, five light cruisers, seven destroyers, three escort destroyers, and three corvettes. The third-largest national force was the Free French Navy (*Forces Navales Françaises Libres*), commanded by Contre-Amiral Robert Jaujard, which contributed two light cruisers, two frigates, and three corvettes. Additionally, despite being heavily committed in the eastern sector, the Royal Canadian Navy would provide a corvette and ten minesweepers off Omaha. Even the Royal Netherlands Navy (*Koninklijke Marine*) contributed a gunboat to Utah.

Scores of auxiliary craft were supplied by Britain or the Commonwealth. Indeed, the Commonwealth provided many landing ships and "furnished a large majority of minecraft, many specialized types of small craft, and all the Fairmile motor launches and danbuoy layers."[1] These many British transports and auxiliaries were typically operated not by the Royal Navy but by the British Merchant Navy flying the Red Ensign.

---

1 *The Invasion of France and Germany,* Naval Institute Press (2011)

Warships

Allied combat aircraft could reach Normandy from southwest England, meaning no aircraft carriers were required in the WNTF. However, three very old US battleships were assigned late in the planning process. The newest was the 27,500-ton battleship *Nevada*, mounting ten 14in./45 guns and commissioned in 1916. It was accompanied by the 27,000-ton battleship *Texas*, also mounting ten 14in./45 guns but commissioned in 1914. The third battleship was the ancient 26,000-ton *Arkansas*, mounting 12 12in./50 guns and commissioned in 1912. Reinforcing the US battleships was the 7,200-ton Royal Navy monitor HMS *Erebus*, commissioned in 1916 and armed with two 15in. guns. Together, these four warships boasted 34 battleship-caliber guns.

The World War I-era battlewagons were augmented by four heavy cruisers. The newest was the USN's 13,600-ton Baltimore-class heavy cruiser USS *Quincy*, commissioned in December 1943 and mounting nine 8in./55 and 12 5in./38 guns. Next were two USN treaty cruisers commissioned in the early 1930s: the 9,975-ton New Orleans-class USS *Tuscaloosa* (nine 8in./55 and eight 5in./25 guns) and the 9,050-ton Northampton-class USS *Augusta* (eight 8in./55 and eight 5in./25 guns). The oldest heavy cruiser present was the ancient 9,800-ton HMS *Hawkins*, commissioned in 1919 and mounting seven 7.5in. and four 4in. guns. All three US vessels could reach 33 knots, 4 knots faster than *Hawkins*. Together, the four heavy cruisers brought 33 7.5in. and 8in. guns to bear on the Normandy coast, equivalent to 16 US Army 8in. heavy artillery batteries.

Battleship *Nevada* bombards Utah on June 6, 1944. *Nevada* famously got underway during the Pearl Harbor attack before being ordered to scuttle itself near the channel entrance. *Nevada* was raised within a few months and spent much of 1942 getting fully refurbished. (NHHC 80-G-231961)

USS *Charles Carroll* (APA-28) was a Crescent City-class attack transport commissioned on August 13, 1942. It is seen on May 6, 1943, after the removal of its after 5in./51 gun and its replacement by two twin 40mm AA guns. (US Navy 80-G-66352)

Four British and two French light cruisers were assigned to the WNTF. The 9,100-ton Town-class HMS *Glasgow* (1937) and 7,580-ton Emerald-class HMS *Enterprise* (1926) mounted batteries of 12 6in. and eight 4in. guns (*Glasgow*) and seven 6in. and eight 4in. guns (*Enterprise*). Accompanying them were HMS *Bellona* and HMS *Black Prince*, two 5,950-ton Dido-class light cruisers mounting eight 5.4in. guns and newly commissioned in autumn 1943. The Free French provided the 7,600-ton La Galissonnière-class light cruisers *Montcalm* and *Georges Leygues*, both commissioned in 1937. Each mounted nine 6in./55 guns and eight 3.5in. antiaircraft guns. Nominal top speed for all six light cruisers was 31–33 knots. An outlier, the 1,457-ton Dutch gunboat HNLMS *Soemba*, mounted three light cruiser-sized 5.9in. (150mm) guns, plus one 75mm gun. Commissioned in 1926, *Soemba* made only 15 knots.

The Americans, British, French, and Canadians contributed 50 destroyers, destroyer-escorts, frigates, and corvettes to the WNTF. Five brand-new US Allen M. Sumner-class destroyers deployed with the Utah escort group. However, the remaining US destroyers, assigned first to escort groups and then to the beaches, were of the 1,630-ton Gleaves class, which could make 37 knots and mounted four 5in./38 guns each. The Gleaves were accompanied by six 1,740-ton Buckley-class destroyer-escorts, which made 24 knots and mounted three 3in./50 guns, plus five British escort destroyers of the 1,087-ton Hunt Type III. The Hunts had a top speed of 27 knots and were armed with four 4in. guns. The French contributed two 1,370-ton River-class frigates, each mounting two 4in. guns and capable of 20 knots. In addition, six 925-ton, 16-knot Flower-class corvettes (three French, two British, and one Canadian) served with the WNTF as escorts and mounted one 4in. gun each. The Flowers were accompanied by the ancient British destroyer HMS *Boadicea*, effectively a seventh corvette.

The landings' direct and indirect fire support would have to come from the WNTF until sufficient US Army artillery could come ashore and get organized. However, the available firepower was not a problem. Even not including the 34 heavy battleship guns, Kirk's warships assigned to bombardment duty provided the rough US Army equivalent of 16 8in. batteries, five 155mm battalions, and fifteen 105mm battalions.

Transports and landing ships

In April 1943, the troopship USS *Ancon* (AP-66) was converted into a Combined Headquarters and Communication ship (AGC) and redesignated AGC-4. Displacing 14,150 tons in its command role, *Ancon* would serve as Hall's Force O flagship directing the Omaha assault.

The WNTF employed eight US attack transports (APA) from several different classes. Attack transports carried 1,500–1,650 assault troops each and were too large and valuable to be risked near shore. Some were converted prewar liners, but most were wartime constructions adapted from the US Maritime

Commission's many standardized civilian designs; these latter types averaged around 16,000 tons fully loaded. As H-Hour approached, attack transports would lower up to 24 empty LCVPs (Landing Craft, Vehicles and Personnel) or other landing craft into the water. Heavily laden assault troops would then climb down cargo netting laid over the side and embark into the bobbing landing craft as carefully as possible.

Preparing for D-Day, US combat equipment is loaded onto USS LST-357 in England in late May or early June 1944. An ambulance backs through the LST's open clamshell bow doors. An outboard motor destined for a Rhino pontoon ferry is in the foreground, while a jeep lurks in the left background. (NHHC USA C-708)

Averaging 15,000 tons fully loaded, the USN's conventional transports (AP) were more strictly "troop transports" because they lacked the attack transports' intrinsic landing craft, as well as their heavier antiaircraft batteries. The WNTF employed three US troopships.

The Royal Navy called its attack transport types Landing Ship, Infantry, or LSI. The Landing Ship, Infantry (Large), or LSI(L), carried 24 LCAs (Landing Craft, Assault). Those LSI(L)s assigned to the WNTF had been built in the United States and were based on US Maritime Commission hull designs. In addition to the LSI(L)s, two smaller LSI types served with the WNTF. These were the Landing Ship, Infantry (Small), designated LSI(S), and the Landing Ship, Infantry (Hand-hoisting), LSI(H).

The WNTF also employed a single example of two different amphibious ship types. The first was the WNTF's lone attack cargo ship (AKA), the 6,761-ton Andromeda-class USS *Achernar* (AKA-53). Faster and more heavily armed than a standard freighter, attack cargo ships transported combat-loaded freight and vehicles, which they delivered ashore via landing craft. The second type was the 4,032-ton Casa Grande-class dock landing ship (LSD) HMS *Oceanway*. As a dock landing ship, *Oceanway*'s floodable well deck supported multiple large landing craft for quickly shuttling tanks and other vehicles ashore.

The 328ft Landing Ship, Tank, or LST, displaced 1,800 tons empty but could land directly on the beach and unload 20 M4 Sherman medium tanks or equivalent vehicles over a ramp extending from its opened bow. An LST boasted a 211-man crew and sported up to eight 40mm guns and 12 20mm guns. Each US LST at Normandy also towed a Rhino ferry (detailed below). The WNTF employed 121 LSTs off Utah and Omaha.

Despite its designation, the 246-ton, 158ft Landing Craft, Infantry (Large), or LCI(L), was essentially a shore-to-shore landing ship. Originally developed by the British to land company-sized follow-up waves, the LCI(L) could deliver 188 troops or 75 tons of cargo ashore. It had a crew of 29 and was armed with five 20mm guns.

Auxiliary Minesweeper USS *Auk* (AM-57) off Virginia's Norfolk Navy Yard in May 1942, wearing Measure 12 (modified) camouflage. Commissioned in January 1942, *Auk* was the lead member of the eponymous class. Like many of its feathered namesakes, USS *Auk* served off Normandy on June 6, 1944. (NH 84027)

TECHNICAL FACTORS
Auxiliaries

In addition to the larger and more glamorous warships and transports, large, complex amphibious assaults required scores of diverse auxiliary vessels. Among the most important were minesweepers. US minesweepers were of the 890-ton Auk class and 810-ton Raven class. These 18-knot vessels mounted two 3in./50 guns. British and Canadian minesweepers were of the 672-ton Bangor class and mounted a 3in. or 4in. gun.

Naval trawlers of about 550 tons resembled fishing trawlers but were fitted for various auxiliary naval uses. Some functioned as danlayers, laying lighted dan buoys to mark mineswept channels. Others were improvised minesweepers. The WNTF employed scores of British 112ft Fairmile motor launches, versatile 75-ton coastal defense vessels used as control craft and navigation leaders. Many tugs also accompanied the WNTF, including ten oceangoing V-4 tugs manned by the US Merchant Marine. Another 18 tugs were crewed by the US Army Transport Service for towing barges across the Channel and positioning Mulberry blockships for scuttling.

Sixty 83ft USCG cutters were piggybacked across the Atlantic and designated Rescue Flotilla 1. Of these, 30 were assigned to the WNTF. Nicknamed the "Matchbox Fleet" for their wood construction and large gasoline tanks, the cutters would rescue 157 men off Utah and 194 off Omaha.

Led by Lieutenant-Commander John D. Bulkeley, 30 US PT Boats in three squadrons would participate at Normandy, although only the 12 Elco boats of 34 Squadron arrived in time for D-Day. Accompanying the Americans were about 12 British motor torpedo boats.

Throughout June 1944, some 326 cargo ships would carry freight and troops to both the American and British zones in Normandy. Some 200 ships were American, and 194 were Liberty ships. Armed with a 4in. gun and an antiaircraft battery, a 14,245-ton Liberty ship could carry 480 men and 120 vehicles at 11 knots. Liberty ships were equipped with cranes to unload their cargo onto waiting landing craft, which would then carry the supplies to shore. Another valuable type was the coaster, merchantmen designed purely for coastal transport. Although small and shallow-drafted, coasters were perfectly adequate for cross-Channel operations and could often safely beach at high tide.

Gunfire support craft

With major USN gunships added so late to *Neptune*, US planners desperately sought methods to increase their seemingly inadequate naval gunfire support. This inspired the USN's first use of British-style Gunfire Support Craft. Most had been built in the United States as LCTs and donated to the Royal Navy under Lend-Lease, then been converted into specialized gunfire support craft by the British, before finally being donated back to the USN as reverse Lend-Lease. As such, they often mounted British weapons and equipment.

US Army M4 Sherman medium tanks and other equipment of the US 741st Tank Battalion, destined for Omaha, loaded aboard an LCT in England in late May or early June 1944. USS LCT-213 is tied up alongside, while several LSTs are visible anchored further out into the harbor. It should be noted that these Shermans are equipped with the deep snorkels and are therefore "wading" tanks rather than the "swimming" DD-equipped Shermans that would shortly become infamous. (NHHC USA C-724)

The Landing Craft, Tank (Armored), or LCT(A), was an LCT fitted with armored plating and converted to allow two of its embarked M4 Sherman tanks to fire over the bow ramp while the vessel was still en route to the beach. Tank fire would commence about H-15 (H-Hour minus 15 minutes), or when their designated targets were within 3,000yds. After beaching, disgorging their tanks, and retracting, LCT(A)s were to return to the Transport Area and join the Ferry Service. Eight LCT(A)s deployed at Utah and eight at Omaha. The similar Landing Craft, Tank (High Explosive), or LCT(HE), carried self-propelled M7 Priest 105mm howitzers, which fired from between 8,000 and 3,000yds from the beach. No LCT(HE) were employed at Utah, but there were ten at Omaha. Additionally, each LCT(A) and LCT(HE) towed a Landing Craft, Mechanized, or LCM, for the gapping teams.

The Landing Craft, Tank (Rocket), or LCT(R), was filled with launchers loaded with 1,080 3ft-long, 5in.-wide, 60lb rockets. An LCT(R) could launch all 32.5 tons of rockets within 90 seconds, but could only be aimed by pointing the entire LCT(R) at the target. There were five LCT(R)s off Utah and nine at Omaha. While psychologically impressive, the LCT(R) proved wholly inaccurate at shore bombardment.

The Landing Craft, Gun (Large), or LCG(L), was armed with two 47mm guns and a 20mm Oerlikon antiaircraft battery. There were four LCG(L)s at Utah and five at Omaha.

A Landing Craft, Flak, or LCF, was an LCT converted to carry antiaircraft batteries. LCF armament varied; a sample configuration comprised 2-pdr pom-poms and ten double 20mm Oerlikons. The LCFs guarded the flanks of the boat channels from the line of departure to close inshore. Because no

An excellent view of diverse *Neptune* assault shipping. In the foreground are two fully loaded *Joseph T. Dickman* LCVPs, the USN's workhorse assault landing craft. Behind them is Rhino pontoon barge RB-24, fully loaded with ambulance trucks; behind the Rhino is LCT-489. In the deep left background are several assorted freighters, while in the far right there appear to be LSTs. This image is from June 14, 1944, as US troops put ashore at the Baie de Seine in Normandy. (US Coast Guard NARA ID 205578585, Local ID 26-G-2414)

Luftwaffe attacks materialized against the Americans, the four LCFs at Utah and seven at Omaha settled for opportunistic attacks against enemy bunkers and machine-gun positions.

The six-man, 36ft Landing Craft, Small (Support), or LCS(S), was armed with 12 rockets, several machine guns, and eight stern-mounted MkIII smoke pots. The LCS(S) craft would help lead the initial assault wave to the beach, close to 300yds, lay smoke, and then provide direct fire support before reporting to the Patrol Craft, or PCs, to function as guides or dispatch vessels. Their crews nicknamed them "Landing Craft, Suicide Squad."

Immediately before the landings, adapted LCP(L) craft called LCP(L) Smoke would lay smokescreens to cover the incoming assault waves. A total of 32 LCP(L) Smoke were assigned to Omaha and 20 to Utah.

Assault beaches and landing craft

Utah and Omaha were subdivided into specific beaches codenamed by phonetic letter and color. For example, Utah was subdivided into Beach Uncle Red to the left and Beach Tare Green to the right (hereafter referred to simply as Beach Red and Beach Green). Each of these smaller beaches represented a battalion-sized landing front.

The transports would anchor 11 nautical miles (nm) from shore, putting them over the horizon from German heavy artillery. The various US landing craft types averaged 9–11 knots at best. The subsequent long landing craft run-in would therefore badly stress and demoralize the assault troops, who would be forced to endure wet and chilly spray, heavy chop, seasickness, and the prolonged tension of nervously imagining their impending fate.

Control craft were vital in marshaling and guiding landing craft and gun-equipped fire support craft to their assigned landing zones, as well as coordinating and controlling post-landing tasks such as supply buildup and casualty withdrawals. Among these vessels were steel-hulled Patrol Craft (PC), which were 175ft long, weighed 280 tons, and made 20 knots. They mounted a 3in. gun as well as considerable specialized navigation equipment. The smaller, wooden-hulled submarine chasers (SCs) were 110ft-long, 20-knot anti-submarine vessels also armed with a 3in. gun and assigned control duties. Modified 56ft Landing Craft, Control, or LCC, vessels were specially equipped for navigation and communication, including a 15–20nm range SO surface search radar. LCCs were intended to find lanes swept free of obstacles and naval mines, and then safely guide successive waves of landing craft into the beach. Four LCCs each were deployed at Utah and Omaha.

As dawn broke, the Americans would land three Regimental Combat Teams (RCTs) ashore, with the US 8th RCT (4th Infantry Division) assaulting Utah and the 16th RCT (1st Infantry Division) and 116th RCT (29th Infantry Division) hitting Omaha. By afternoon, additional waves would reinforce the original three RCTs to six such teams. An RCT was a 3,257-man US infantry regiment specially augmented for an amphibious assault. Its three Battalion Landing Teams (BLTs) were expected to land across a regimental beach front 3,000yds wide. Each BLT comprised three reinforced 215-man infantry companies, each of which was carried ashore by seven LCVPs (six assault boats and one special command boat). Typically, two BLTs would land abreast, with the third following as a reserve.

Attached to each of the dawn assault RCTs was a tank battalion specially outfitted for amphibious assaults. The assault's intended first landing wave would comprise Duplex Drive or DD Tanks. These M4 Sherman medium tanks, heavily modified to "swim," would be launched 5,000yds out by specialized LCT vessels. A collapsible watertight canvas floatation screen and supplemental propellers gave DD tanks a nominal 3ft freeboard and 4-knot speed under favorable conditions, but their actual seaworthiness was quite suspect. Of a tank battalion's three medium tank companies, two comprised swimming DD tanks, while the third (reserve) company comprised Shermans merely outfitted with wading trunks and watertight sealant; these Shermans could wade in turret-deep water. A tank battalion's light tank company (M5 Stuarts) and the battalion headquarters would arrive in landing craft during the afternoon of D-Day.

Immediately following the DD tanks would be the official first wave of landing craft, carrying engineers and infantry. The United States' primary landing craft by 1944 was the 36ft Landing Craft, Vehicles and Personnel. Manned by a crew of three, an LCVP mounted two 0.30-caliber machine guns and could carry 36 troops to shore at 12 knots. Alternatively, it could carry either a light gun, 5 tons of cargo, or a 1-ton truck and 12 troops. The LCVP was carried (often nested in other landing craft) aboard other ships, such as attack transports, and then lowered empty into the water before being loaded. In addition to the infantry and engineers were the US 2nd and 5th Ranger Battalions of 524 men each. Rangers rode the LCA, the British counterpart to the LCVP. An LCA also carried 36 troops and differed from the LCVP in certain details.

Following immediately behind the assault companies' LCVPs would be LCI(L)s (detailed above) containing specific RCT attachments, such as Engineer Combat Battalions, Naval Combat Battalions, and the corresponding Divisional Headquarters. A Gap Assault Team (GAT) combined a 28-man US Army engineer team with a 13-man Naval Combat Demolition Unit. With the help of an attached Sherman tank dozer, each GAT was expected to blow a 50yd-wide lane through beach obstructions before high tide arrived.

The four-man, 26-ton, 56ft-long Landing Craft, Mechanized, or LCM(6), could carry either one light tank, one medium gun, 75 troops, or 35 tons of cargo. Each LCM(6) was armed with two 0.50-caliber machine guns. LCM(6)s were usually employed to land trucks directly onto the beach.

The larger 13-man, 133-ton, 119ft-long Landing Craft, Tank, or LCT(6), could carry either nine trucks, four M4 Sherman medium tanks, 150 troops, or 150 tons of cargo. It was armed with two 20mm and two 0.50-caliber guns. LCT(6)s were primarily used in follow-up waves to land multiple tanks directly ashore.

Using Utah as an example, a total of 26 assault waves were scheduled to land at 10–20-minute intervals, beginning at H-Hour, until just before noon. The first 12 waves would overwhelmingly be landing craft, while the next 14 waves would comprise larger, heavier beaching craft.

Logistic craft and vehicles

Adapted from the CCKW 2.5-ton truck, the one-man, 31ft-long DUKW amphibious truck could carry 24 troops or 2.5 tons of cargo. The DUKW could make six knots in the water, and its 6x6 drivetrain could reach 50mph on dry land. The DUKW was not a combat vehicle but was essential for logistic operations immediately following an amphibious assault. The DUKW was particularly prized because it could deliver small-level cargo directly from the ship to its final location inland without the additional wasted time, manpower, and equipment required to unload and reload at the shoreline.

Lighters (called dumb barges by the US Army) were simply large unpowered steel barges used to transport vehicles and stores, and were towed across the Channel. Six were beached in the assault area on D-Day, as a 1,500-ton capacity barge could supply an infantry division with ammunition for two days. Post-action reports lavishly praised the barges' utility, remarking that they had been underexploited. Had more ships been available for towing, the barges could have made multiple round trips.

Rhino ferries were 175ft-long, 43ft-wide, 5ft-deep self-propelled pontoon barges that could unload on nearly any gradient. Although two 160hp outboard motors powered them up to 5 knots, they were usually towed across the Channel by LSTs. Rhino ferries had six times the capacity of an LCT and ten times that of an LCVP; two Rhinos could empty an LST. A common Rhino load was a DUKW and a bulldozer, both lashed down.

Western Naval Task Force air support

Air cover for *Neptune* would be provided by Air Chief Marshal Sir Trafford Leigh-Mallory's Allied Expeditionary Air Force, based in Britain and numbering 7,537 combat aircraft (3,191 heavy bombers, 467 medium bombers, 393 light bombers, and 3,486 fighters). Of these, the Royal Air Force (RAF) provided 957 heavy bombers, 237 light bombers, and 1,306 fighters (2,500 in total), while the US Eighth Air Force contributed 2,234 heavy bombers and 903 fighters (3,137 in total).

Additionally, flying in direct air support of the WNTF was Lieutenant-General Lewis H. Brereton's US Ninth Air Force of 467 medium bombers,

156 light bombers, and 1,277 fighters (1,900 in total). US Army Air Support Parties were assigned to land with each RCT, as well as each Division and Corps headquarters. Each Air Support Party was equipped with vehicle-mounted VHF and HF radio sets to facilitate tactical air support.

The RAF would provide low-level fighter cover over the beaches, the USAAF (US Army Air Forces) IX Fighter Command would provide high cover, and long-range P-38s would patrol over the Channel. To avoid friendly fire, Allied aircraft were painted with distinctive D-Day "invasion stripes," while aircraft recognition officers were attached to each warship.

To discourage low-level enemy air attacks, barrage balloons were carried by every LCI as well as some larger ships. After H-Hour, the WNTF would fly barrage balloons at 1,000ft altitude. When visibility fell below 1,500yds or the cloud ceiling below 1,000ft, the balloons would be flown at 300ft. However, many barrage balloons were quickly cut loose, as they provided German artillery with the locations of US ships that were otherwise over the horizon.

The American buildup in Britain, 1943–44

The transatlantic buildup of American troops to Britain, Operation *Bolero*, had begun in April 1942 with the expectation of invading France in autumn 1942 (*Sledgehammer*) or summer 1943 (*Roundup*). To support *Sledgehammer* or *Roundup*, on May 24, 1942, the US Army established the Service of Supply (SOS) for the European Theater of Operations (ETO). However, *Sledgehammer/Roundup* was effectively scuttled in July 1942 in favor of Northwest Africa's Operation *Torch*. Nevertheless, on January 22, 1943, the Combined Chiefs of Staff (CCS) established the office of COSSAC (Chief of Staff of the Supreme Allied Commander), under the British Lieutenant-General Frederick E. Morgan. COSSAC's assignment was to "prepare a detailed appreciation and outline plan for cross channel operations on the assumption that this operation [the invasion of France] would take place in 1944."[2] COSSAC's directive partially restored the importance of a US troop buildup in Britain, evolving the nearly defunct Operation *Bolero* into a joint Army-Navy shipping program in March 1943.

The May 12–25, 1943, Washington Conference (TRIDENT) would tentatively approve COSSAC's plan to invade Northwest Europe, called *Overlord*, for May 1944. However, only conditional approval of *Overlord* was given at the subsequent August 1943 Quebec Conference (QUADRANT).

A US Army halftrack antiaircraft vehicle backs through the open well deck of a US LCT in southern England in late May or early June 1944. Despite long-held fears about Luftwaffe attacks, the US Army's extensive antiaircraft assets hardly had a job to do and were more often put to use in the infantry support role. (NHHC USA C-751)

Nevertheless, on August 21, 1943, the CCS approved COSSAC's Appreciation and Outline Plan, and despite British reluctance, ordered COSSAC to begin extensive invasion preparations. At the November 1943 Tehran Conference (EUREKA), Roosevelt maneuvered the British into a firm commitment to *Overlord* for 1944. The November 18, 1943, CCS 398[3] declared: "Operation *Overlord* will be the primary U.S.-British ground and air effort against Germany (in 1944)."

Although COSSAC had laid the groundwork for *Overlord* , including the *Neptune* invasion site of Normandy, it was now dissolved and replaced by the newly established Supreme Headquarters Allied Expeditionary Forces (SHAEF). The US Army's General Dwight D. Eisenhower was named SHAEF commander on December 24, 1943 and Allied preparations for *Overlord* started picking up immediately. American strength in Britain began accumulating rapidly; the Cunard liners *Queen Mary* and *Queen Elizabeth* alone could each transport up to 15,000 US troops per crossing – the manpower of an entire US infantry division. Additionally, from November 1943 through February 1944, *Bolero* would ship an average of 320 million tons of supplies per month to Britain. By March 1944, this figure would soar to 506 million tons before peaking at 659 million tons during the invasion month of June.

US troop convoys to the United Kingdom disembarked in Great Britain's western ports and were thus assembled on the western and southwestern counties of the island. From this it naturally followed that the Americans would comprise the western flank of the Normandy assault. However, by May 1944, a transatlantic shipping backlog had developed, with the New York Port of Embarkation informed that only 120 more ships could be accepted at British ports; this was despite New York's own *Overlord* shipping backlog of 540,000 tons, for which New York was short 61 ships anyway. Nevertheless, by May 31, 1944, US Army ground forces in Britain available for *Overlord* comprised 12 infantry divisions, five armored divisions, two airborne divisions, five armored groups, and two Ranger battalions.

US TROOPS AND SUPPLIES IN UK, JANUARY 1942 – MAY 1944		
Date	Total US troops in United Kingdom	Total US tons of supplies and equipment in United Kingdom
January 31, 1942	4,058	108
July 31, 1942	81,273	181,979
January 31, 1943	122,097	881,554
July 31, 1943	238,028	1,492,757
January 31, 1944	937,308	3,497,761
May 30, 1944	1,526,965	5,297,306

---

3   Combined Chiefs of Staff 398

HOW THE FLEET OPERATED

DOCTRINE, COMMAND, AND COMMUNICATION

The full *Neptune* invasion fleet was commanded by Allied Naval Commander-in-Chief Expeditionary Force (ANCFX) Admiral Sir Bertram Ramsay (RN). Ramsay's US subordinate, Force O commander Rear Admiral Hall, recalled Ramsay as "quiet, brilliant, intelligent, determined and easy to get along with."[4] On February 28, 1944, Ramsay issued the Naval Outline Plan for *Overlord* . According to WNTF commander Kirk: "All the planning was done in Norfolk House by Admiral Ramsay and his staff in the minutest detail." *Neptune* comprised the two assault forces in the American-commanded WNTF, plus the three assault forces in the British-commanded Eastern Naval Task Force (ENTF).

Neptune's ground component was the Anglo-American 21st Army Group, commanded by the British Army's General Sir Bernard Montgomery. This force was divided into the British 2nd Army in the east, under Lieutenant-General Sir Miles Dempsey, and the First US Army in the west, under Lieutenant-General Omar Bradley. A planned third force, the Third US Army, under Lieutenant-General George S. Patton, would be activated in Normandy three weeks

Allied staff observe *Neptune* operations ashore from the Western Naval Task Force flagship, heavy cruiser USS *Augusta*, on June 8, 1944. From left to right: Rear Admiral Alan G. Kirk, Lieutenant-General Omar Bradley, Rear Admiral Arthur D. Struble (with binoculars), and Major General William B. Kean. (Public Domain)

4   USN Admin Vol 5 Operation *Neptune*

after D-Day. Bradley would then be "kicked upstairs" to command the planned US 12th Army Group, with First US Army and Third US Army subordinated within.

Very late on D-1 (D-Day minus one), the US 101st and 82nd Airborne Divisions would airdrop several miles behind the Utah beaches to secure causeways across lowlands that SHAEF expected the Germans to flood. Several hours later, on the morning of D-Day, Kirk's WNTF would land Bradley's First US Army on the western Normandy beaches. Rear Admiral Moon's Force U would land the vanguard of Major-General J. Lawton Collins' US VII Corps (US 4th Division) on the Cotentin peninsula at Utah, while Rear Admiral Hall's Force O would simultaneously land the vanguard of Major-General Leonard T. Gerow's US V Corps (US 1st Division and US 29th Division) at Omaha. Force U and Force O were of roughly equal size; together they expected to land 60,000 men and 6,800 vehicles in the morning's initial assault phase.

ASSAULT FORCES U AND O

Rear Admiral Moon's Assault Force U (Task Force 125) was organized into 16 Task Groups

Landing Force	TG-125.1	Major General Collins, US Army VII Corps, Major General Barton, US Army 4th Infantry Division and attached units.
Shore Party	TG-125.2	1st Engineer Special Brigade - Brigadier General Wharton US Army.
Force Flagship	TG-125.3	USS *Bayfield*, Capt. Lynden Spencer, USCG.
Green Assault Group	TG-125.4	Cmdr. A.L. Warburton, USN, in LCH 530. 1 APA, 1 LSI(L), 15 LST, 23 LCI(L), 1 LCH, 69 LCT, 26 LCM, 3 RHF, 1 PC, 2 LCG.
Red Assault Group	TG-125.5	Comdr. E.W. Wilson, USNR, in LCH 10. 2 APA, 15 LST, 22 LCI(L), 1 LCH, 83 LCT, 25 LCM, 2 RHF, 1 PC, 2 LCG.
Escorts	TG-125.6	7 D.D. 3 A/S Trawlers, 2 Corvettes, 7 PC, 7 SC, 4 ML, 3 970 MLs.
Support Craft Group	TG-125.7	Lt. Comdr. L.E. Hart, USNR, in LCH 209, 4 LCG(L), 5 LCT(R), 12 LCS(S), 4 LCS, 8 LCT(A), 16 LCP(L).
Bombardment Group	TG-125.8	R.Adm. M.L. Deyo, USN, in USS *Tuscaloosa*, 2 CA, 1 OBB, 1 BM, 2 CL, 1 OCA, 1 PG, 8 DD.
Minesweeper Group	TG-125.9	Comdr. M.H. Brown, RN, (in HMS *Shippigan*), 16 MS, 11 AM, 18 YMS, 9 MHS, 8 ML, 8 Danlayers, 3 HDML Miscellaneous units as assigned.
Far Shore Service Group (NOIC-UTAH)	TG-125.10	Capt. J.R. Arnold USNR, 2 LHK, 14 Pontoon Causeways, 8 Blisters, 2 Warping Tugs, 1 Repair Barge, 1 LCH, 6 RHF, 22 LCM(3), 36 LBV (2) 1 ARL, 8 LBE, 5 Fueling Trawlers, 20 LBO, 3 LBW.
Sea Rescue Group	TG-125.11	Comdr. Stewart, USCG, T5 10 Coast Guard Cutters.
Follow-up Convoy Group	TG-125.12	Comdr. W.S. Blair, USNR. 25 LST.
PT Boats	TG-125.13	R.R. Reed, USNR. 13 PT
Special Task Groups	TG-125.14	Lt.Comdr. H.M. Ness, RNVR. 7 HDML
Combat Salvage and Fire Fighting Unit "U"	TG-122.3.2	Lt.Comdr. M.L. McClung, USNR. 2 AT, 1 ATR.
Causeway Construction Unit	TG-125.15	Lt.Comdr. Bains, USNR

Rear Admiral Hall's Assault Force O (Task Force 124) was organized into 13 Task Groups:		
Landing Force	TG-124.1	Major General Huebner, USA 1st US Inf. Div. (less 26th RCT, plus 115th & 116th RCTs of the 29th Inf. Div., plus 2nd & 5th Ranger Batts) Reinforced.
Shore Party	TG-124.2	Brigadier General Hoge, USA 2/3ds 5th Engr. Special Brigade; 2/3ds 6th US Naval Beach Batt; 1/3d 6th Engr. Special Brigade; 1/3d 7th US Naval Beach Batt.
Assault Group O-1	TG-124.3	Capt. Fritzsche, USCG 2 APAs; 1 LCH; 1 LSI(L); 6 LSTs; 5 LCI(L)s; 53 LCTs; 18 LCM(3)s; 2 PCs; 2 SCs; 2 MLs; 2 LCCs.
Assault Group O-2	TG-124.4	Capt. Bailey, USN 2 APAs; 1 LCH; 1 LSI(L); 6 LSTs; 17 LCI(L)s; 54 LCTs; 18 LCM(3)s; 4 PCs; 2 MLs; 4 SCs; 3 LCGs.
Assault Group O-3	TG-124.5	Captain Schulten, USN 3 XAPs; 1 LCH; 12 LSTs; 11 LCI(L)s; 39 LCTs; 1 LSD; 3 PCs; 2 MLs; 3 LSI(S)s; 3 LSI(H)s; 1 LCT(5); 2 MLs.
Escorts	TG-124.6	Captain Sanders, USN 12 US DDs; 3 Hunt DDs; 3 US DE; 2 OODs; 6 SGBs; 2 Frigates; 3 A/S Trawlers; 9 PCs; 6 SCs; 5 MLs (970); 7 MLs; 2 HDMLs; 7 MTBs.
Gunfire Support Craft	TG-124.8	Captain Sabin, USN 1 LCH; 7LCFs; 5 LCG(L)s; 9 LCT(R)s; 28 LCP(L)s; 8 LCT(A)s; 10 LCT(HE)s.
Bombardment Group	TG-124.9	Rear-Admiral Bryant, USN 2 BBs; 3 CLs; 9 US DDs; 3 Hunt DDs
Sweeper Group	TG-124.10	Commander Cochrane, RN 9 MS; 3 Danlayers; 4 MLs; 8 BYMHs; 9 MMs.
Far Shore Service Group OMAHA		1 Accom. Ship; 1 ARL; 12 LCMs; 8 LCI(L)s; 4 LCH; 72 LCT(5) and (6)s; 20 RHFs; 139 LCM(3)s; 72 LBV(2)s; 172 LCVPs; 9 Fuel Trawlers; 16 LBEs; 26 LBCs; 5 LBWs; 2 LBKs; 1 Pont Drydock.
Dispatch Boats	TG-124.12	1 US PT; 9 Disp. Boats.
Rescue Vessels	TG-124.13	15 USCG Cutters.

Naval officers would command at sea and during the run-in. Once a naval vessel or unit had successfully deployed its associated US Army headquarters ashore, the naval commander would cede tactical command to his Army counterpart. For example, as commander of the full WNTF, Kirk would command the whole US invasion until Lieutenant-General Bradley's headquarters was fully established ashore, when command of the American landings would transfer to Bradley.

Beginning the afternoon of D-Day, Commodore Campbell D. Edgar's Follow-up Force B would begin landing 26,500 men and 4,400 vehicles of Major-General Charles H. Corlett's US XIX Corps at Omaha on both D-Day's second tide and D+1 (D-Day plus one) to reinforce US V Corps. Finally, a fourth force, already preloaded with 43,500 men and 6,000 vehicles for both beaches, would cross the English Channel on D+1 and D+2. Altogether, before D-Day, over 130,000 US troops and 17,300 US vehicles were already preloaded and ready to sortie. By D+5, some 226,000 troops in nine US divisions were expected ashore at Utah and Omaha. By D+15, this would increase to 402,600 troops and 11 US divisions.

The Royal Navy's Home Fleet, based in Scapa Flow off northern Scotland, would provide *Neptune* with distant cover against heavy Kriegsmarine units. Protection of the fleet's flanks against enemy light units and U-boats would be

Rear Admiral Don P. Moon, circa 1944. Moon was born in Kokomo, Indiana, and in 1916 graduated fourth in his Naval Academy class with an emphasis on gunnery. Moon served on three battleships in the 1920s, but as he moved his way up he commanded destroyers and cruisers. As Force U commander, Moon was responsible for the Slapton Sands disaster. Transferred to southern France after D-Day, Moon found that he was suffering from lingering battle fatigue, a pain Moon ultimately chose to end with his own service pistol on August 5, 1944.

provided by the three Royal Navy Home Commands out of Plymouth, Portsmouth, and Dover. Each Home Command averaged about four destroyers and between six and ten motor torpedo boats for night patrols, with day patrols provided by aircraft.

Directly supporting Moon's Assault Force U at Utah was Rear Admiral Morton L. Deyo's Bombardment Force A. Meanwhile, directly supporting Hall's Assault Force O at Omaha was Rear Admiral Carleton F. Bryant's Bombardment Force C. Additionally, a reserve fire support group was organized to relieve bombardment ships that had depleted their ammunition or suffered significant damage. Assigned to this pool was the WNTF flagship, the heavy cruiser *Augusta*, along with British light cruiser *Bellona* and 17 additional destroyers of US DesDiv-18 (Destroyer Division 18), DesDiv-33, and DesDiv-119. Bombardment ships would report to Portsmouth, Plymouth, or Portland to replenish their ammunition. Destroyers no longer needed for bombardment would be reassigned to area defense of the assault area.

For naval air spotting, it was decided Normandy would be too well defended for the usual slow, vulnerable floatplanes, and would instead require fast and evasive fighters. Britain would provide five Spitfire and Mustang squadrons from the RAF, plus four Seafire squadrons from the Royal Navy. Of the 104 fighters available, 17 would be flown by pilots of the USN's seaplanes; the rest would be flown by British fighter pilots untrained in spotting.

The WNTF had over 40 ships equipped with the US Army's SCR-608 radio equipment for communication with Shore Fire Control parties. Nevertheless, US Army planners greatly feared "blue-on-blue" incidents and imposed severe restrictions on naval gunfire support. According to Commander Utah Gunfire Support Group: "Reports indicate that where assault troop commanders are willing to accept a risk of some danger to their personnel, in order to have sustained fire not only during the approach to the beach, but as they progress inland that, actually, casualties are substantially lower."

INTELLIGENCE AND DECEPTION

Security for *Overlord* was so intense that a security level above Top Secret was created called BIGOT. However, by 1944, most Nazi spies in Britain had already been caught and turned into double-agents under the Double-Cross System. Conversely, the Allies derived much tactical intelligence from RAF and USAAF aerial photoreconnaissance over the Normandy coast. Meanwhile,

ORGANIZATION OF US NAVY *NEPTUNE* FLEET

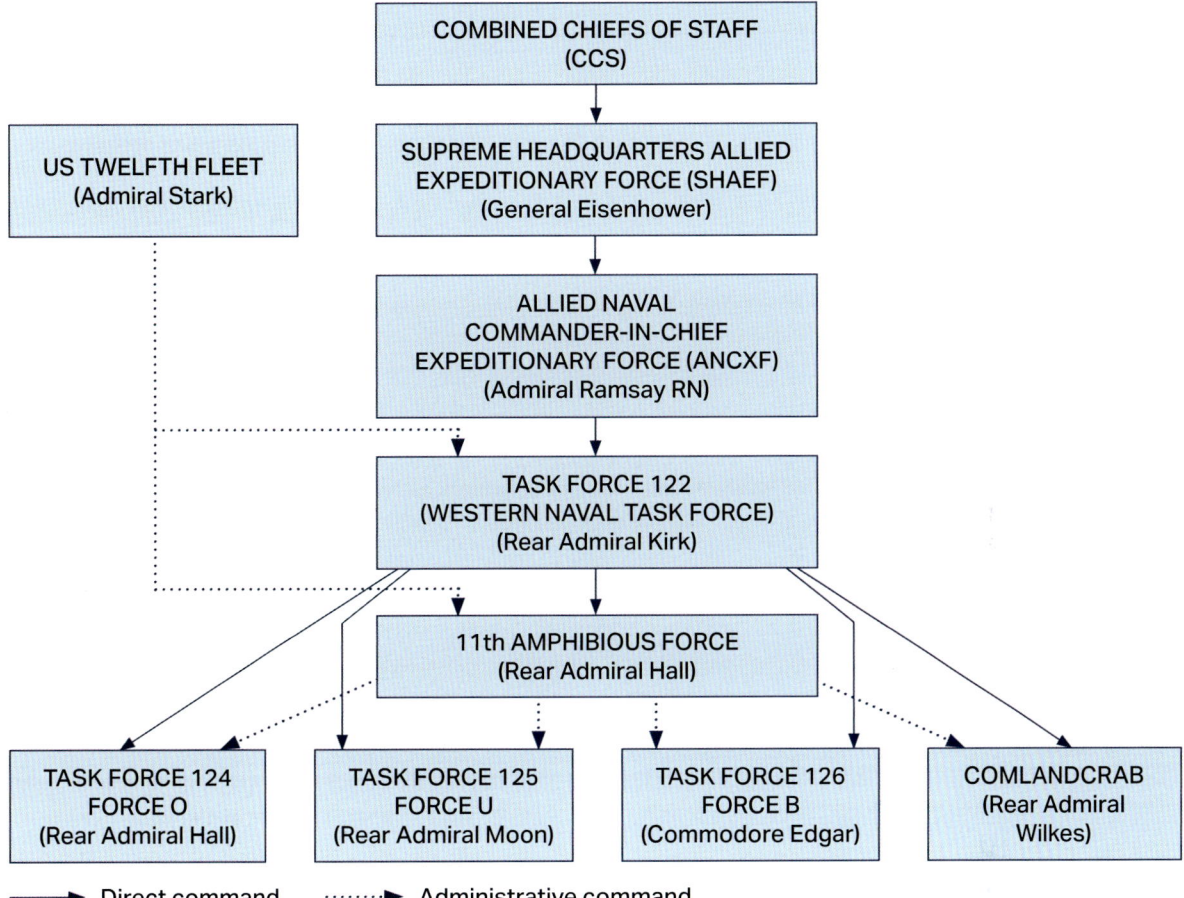

COMBINED CHIEFS OF STAFF (CCS)

US TWELFTH FLEET (Admiral Stark)

SUPREME HEADQUARTERS ALLIED EXPEDITIONARY FORCE (SHAEF) (General Eisenhower)

ALLIED NAVAL COMMANDER-IN-CHIEF EXPEDITIONARY FORCE (ANCXF) (Admiral Ramsay RN)

TASK FORCE 122 (WESTERN NAVAL TASK FORCE) (Rear Admiral Kirk)

11th AMPHIBIOUS FORCE (Rear Admiral Hall)

TASK FORCE 124 FORCE O (Rear Admiral Hall)

TASK FORCE 125 FORCE U (Rear Admiral Moon)

TASK FORCE 126 FORCE B (Commodore Edgar)

COMLANDCRAB (Rear Admiral Wilkes)

→ Direct command   ┄┄► Administrative command

Operation *Overlord/Neptune* was ultimately authorized by the Allied Combined Chiefs of Staff (CCS), which comprised the chiefs of staff of each of the US and British military high commands. The Combined Chiefs of Staff delegated operational command of *Overlord/Neptune* to the Supreme Headquarters Allied Expeditionary Force (SHAEF) which was commanded by US General Dwight D. Eisenhower. SHAEF was a joint Anglo-American command that commanded forces of both nations. However, British/Commonwealth forces are omitted for clarity to focus on *Neptune's* American naval command structure. Also omitted are ground and air forces.

Established on October 1, 1943, the US Navy's Twelfth Fleet, under Admiral Harold Stark, was the administrative command for all US Navy assets allocated to Northwest European waters. All ships, men, and resources required for the US invasion into Normandy were therefore assigned under the Twelfth Fleet umbrella.

The Western Naval Task Force, designated Task Force 122, was established on October 29, 1943 to be the overall at-sea command

of the American part of the invasion and commanded by Rear Admiral Alan G. Kirk. The Western Naval Task Force comprised 2,010 ships and craft.

On August 12, 1943, the 11th Amphibious Force was established under Twelfth Fleet and later the Western Naval Task Force. The 11th Amphibious Force, commanded by Rear Admiral John Hall, was to organize, maintain, and train the forces assigned to the American part of *Neptune*.

On September 1, 1943, the Landing Craft and Bases command (COMLANDCRAB) was established to maintain Twelfth Fleet's assigned bases and landing craft in preparation for and in support of the invasion. COMLANDCRAB was commanded by Rear Admiral John Wilkes.

Within Western Naval Task Force were three major assault forces: Task Force 125 (Force U) hitting Utah, Task Force 124 (Force O) hitting Omaha, and Task Force 125 (Force B), a reinforcement force that would primarily land at Omaha beginning the afternoon of D-Day.

nighttime reconnaissance by British submarines, British MTBs, and US PT Boats would collect buckets of Normandy beach sand to return to Britain for scientific analysis.

According to Rear Admiral Deyo:

> From the Admiralty came a wealth of basic data: depth of water, slope and gradient of the beach at different stages of tide; kind of bottom; strength and direction of current; topography, hydrography; weather; beach exits; roads; terrain and hundreds of items. All down the chain of command flowed a widening stream, digested and sorted by the intelligence sections of various commanders. Large and small monographs and booklets, charts and maps of various scales were being prepared. From Middle Wallop in England the 30th Reconnaissance Squadron USAAF were making almost daily flights to photograph the target area. Their films were studied by expert photo interpreters who revealed their secrets and passed them along to us. This became our most valuable source of information. Transparent overlays for charts and maps were made; on them were placed all enemy gun batteries, strong points and obstacles. These were kept up to date and showed us clearly what awaited us.[5]

British LCA 1377 carries US troops in a May 1944 training exercise prior to D-Day. The "PB" amidships indicates that this LCA belongs to HMS *Prince Baudouin*. The LCA is visibly crewed by British ratings but carrying Americans, most likely US Rangers destined for the Pointe du Hoc assault near Omaha. (NHHC USA C-1087)

Additionally, Allied agents were inserted into France, the first OSS operations using US PT boats taking place during the night of May 19–20, 1944. Finally, thanks to Enigma codebreaking, the Allies had detailed knowledge of the location and scope of German minefields off Normandy, as well as the supposed German order of battle. However, there would be one great D-Day intelligence failure, and that came in the American sector at Omaha.

Operation *Fortitude* was the overall deception effort accompanying *Overlord*. The sub-operation *Fortitude North* would deceive German forces into believing an Allied invasion of Norway was planned for May 1, 1944. *Fortitude*'s most famous element was Operation *Fortitude South*, the sub-operation that specifically targeted the Pas-de-Calais. Indeed, the Wehrmacht (and Hitler personally) had long believed the main Anglo-American invasion would land in the Pas-de-Calais, and assumed any landings at Normandy would be diversionary.

Fortitude South's greatest weapon was the creation of a mythical 150,000-man 1st US Army Group (FUSAG) under Lieutenant-General George S. Patton in southeast England. Although much fake military hardware was assembled opposite the Calais beaches, it was the cleverly simulated FUSAG radio traffic that proved most effective at fooling the

---

5 *Naval Guns at Normandy* by Vice Admiral Morton L. Deyo

German high command. According to SHAEF chief-of-staff Lieutenant-General Walter Bedell Smith: "Those devices were largely the result of British ingenuity, and I came to recognize that the British are masters at this sort of deception."[6]

After the final Fabius dress rehearsal from May 3–8, 1944, the invasion forces maintained strict radio silence, while special radio teams mimicked the real Allied units and emitted radio transmissions suggesting they were in a low and early level of training. Meanwhile, in the weeks leading up to the invasion, the USAAF and RAF pounded the Pas-de-Calais area twice as heavily as Normandy. For example, the formidable Pointe du Hoc position was hit hard on April 15, May 22, and June 4, yet during this period most Allied bombs fell on the French coast north of the Seine and well outside the planned *Neptune* lodgment.

Late on June 5, 1944, minor British air-sea forces would launch three diversionary feints against the French coast away from Normandy. The first, Operation *Glimmer*, involved 18 small vessels comprising 54-ton Harbor Defence Motor Launches (HDML) and RAF Pinnaces. They were supported by chaff-dropping Lancaster bombers of the 617 "Dam Busters" Squadron. Between 0200hrs and 0500hrs on June 6, the 18 vessels loudly broadcast radio traffic and made a high-speed dash to within 2 miles of the Boulogne coast in the Pas-de-Calais area, then retreated under smoke. The second raid, Operation *Taxable*, began at 0100hrs and saw 12 HDMLs similarly feint against Cap d'Antifer, under the cover of six Short Sterling bombers. The third feint, Operation *Big Drum*, targeted Cape (Pointe) Barfleur with four additional HDMLs. According to Ramsay, the radio transmissions and smokescreens emitted by these 38 small craft and their accompanying air support "[gave] an appearance to enemy radar similar to that presented by the real forces. These were very successful … in enabling our forces to continue for so long towards the enemy coast before their composition could be determined."[7]

Ironically, the final, unforeseen decision to launch *Neptune* during a major Channel storm was the most deceptive move of all. By 0800hrs on D-Day, Admiral Theodor Krancke, commander-in-chief of Kriegsmarine Group Command West, would admit: "The enemy have certainly succeeded in surprising to a certain extent the whole machinery of German defense organization, and not least by the clever choice to land when the weather appeared to be unfavorable, but kept improving."[8]

Dwight C. Shepler's Attack on Slapton Sands, a 1944 watercolor depicting one of the Americans' many mock amphibious assaults against Slapton Sands in Devon, England, in preparation for assaulting Utah and Omaha. The area had of course been evacuated before the deep and persistent naval bombardments that opened the assaults. Infantry penetrated inland with flamethrowers and demolitions, while vehicles followed behind them. (NHHC 88-199-dz)

---

6   *USN Admin Vol 5 Operation Neptune*

7   *USN Admin Vol. 5 Operation Neptune*

8   *The Invasion of France and Germany* Naval Institute Press (2011)

LOGISTICS AND FACILITIES
Western Naval Task Force logistics

On July 15, 1943, USN chief Admiral Ernest J. King established Rear Admiral John Wilkes' Landing Craft and Bases Europe command (ComLandCrab) at Falmouth in Cornwall, responsible for landing and beaching craft. On December 17, 1943, the newly established US XI Amphibious Force under Rear Admiral John L. Hall assumed amphibious training and provisioning responsibilities of the WNTF and its assigned US Army formations; Hall would additionally command *Neptune*'s single US assault zone (Omaha). But in March 1944, SHAEF suddenly doubled US assault commitments, forcing the urgent establishment of the new Utah zone and Force U. The WNTF's three main assault commands were now:

Force U at Utah
Force O at Omaha
Follow-Up Force B

Landing Craft and Bases Europe

Kirk assigned the staging and mounting of the WNTF to Commander, Landing Craft and Bases Europe. Ultimately, the WNTF would organize into 24 separate convoys for the initial D-Day assault. Rear Admiral Moon's Force U would load in five ports between Plymouth and Torcross, then sortie in 12 convoys from eight ports between Plymouth and Poole. Rear Admiral Hall's Force O would marshal in Poole and Portland Harbor and cross the English Channel in nine convoys. Commodore Edgar's Follow-up Force B would organize at Falmouth and Fowey before heading to Normandy in three convoys.

SHAEF established the Build-Up Control Organization (BUCO) to handle the first 90 days of Normandy reinforcements. However, Ramsay expected unpredictable delays and alterations once the first troops touched down, and so refused to prescribe convoy schedules past D+3. After four days, Ramsay believed, a natural if unpredictable cross-Channel rhythm would likely have established itself.

British planners had abandoned any direct assault on a harbor after the August 1942 Dieppe disaster. In lieu of a functioning port, planners envisioned a prefabricated harbor, a megaproject codenamed Mulberry that would comprise breakwaters, piers, and causeways, all of which would literally be towed across the Channel in pieces and assembled on the Normandy coast. Long-obsolete ship hulks, or blockships, would be towed into position and scuttled to form breakwaters. Two Mulberries would be established, an American harbor at Omaha (Mulberry A) and a British one at Gold (Mulberry B). Each Mulberry was designed to handle 6,750 tons of supplies a day. Much has been written about the Mulberries; their extensive and fascinating engineering details need not detain us here. The American Mulberry, however, would play a crucial if ironic part in the post-invasion buildup.

Interestingly, LSTs had been successfully landed and unloaded directly on Mediterranean beaches, but the plan forbade this at Normandy, as USN officers feared Normandy's much higher tidal range would break the LSTs' backs.

Final training and rehearsals

Amphibious training was largely carried out in southern England, particularly the Slapton Sands area of Devon. Exercises first began with individual battalions and regiments, before advancing to full divisional and corps maneuvers, including all attached supporting assets, and executed in conjunction with naval and air support. Every effort was made to train in areas under realistic conditions.

In January 1944, Force O participated in three large rehearsals codenamed Duck I, Duck II, and Duck III, followed in March by Exercise Fox. Following these were three smaller training series codenamed Muskrat, Otter, and Mink. Among the requirements was to train landing craft crews to navigate within narrow mineswept channels in strong crosscurrents, and to beach and retract on a flat shore with a large tidal range. According to one US sailor: "We loaded and unloaded various troops and equipment time after time. We were never sure if each practice might be the real thing."

In late March, Moon's newly established Force U executed Exercise Beaver, its first large training operation. Force U's full-scale rehearsal, Exercise Tiger, was to be held between April 24 and 28, 1944. For Tiger, Moon's Force U was expected to mock-invade Slapton Beach, beginning on April 27, to simulate landings at Utah. However, on April 25, Luftwaffe aerial reconnaissance registered the massive fleet concentrating in southwest England for Tiger.

Tiger began poorly on April 27 when a communications foul-up caused US troops to be shelled with live ammunition from their own warships. The tight security and extreme sensitivity of the event means the actual number of friendly fire casualties remains obscure. However, shortly after midnight on April 28, nine German S-boats sortied from Cherbourg. By 0130hrs, they had snuck into Convoy T-4, a Tiger flotilla of eight US LSTs steaming through Lyme Bay and escorted by a single corvette, HMS *Azalea*. Assisted by a tragic Anglo-American farce of miscommunications, misassumptions, and bad luck, the aggressive German S-boats torpedoed three LSTs, inflicting catastrophic losses, and escaped back into the night. Meanwhile, bewildered Allied counterfire could only damage a fourth LST, wounding 18 men.

Rear Admiral John Lesslie Hall, Jr, was the resilient commander of the Omaha assault force. Born in Williamsburg, Virginia, in 1891, Hall played American football for three seasons at William & Mary before transferring to the Naval Academy and playing four more sterling seasons for the Midshipmen. (NH 94034-KN)

Normandy invasion preparations in England during late May or early June 1944. At least one of the beached LCMs is from USS *Samuel Chase* (APA-26). Behind them at the pier are USS LST-374 and USS LST-314; German S-boats would sink LST-314 on June 9. (NHHC USA C-701)

Force U lost two LSTs sunk and two damaged. The 749 Americans killed (551 US Army and 198 US Navy personnel) ultimately exceeded that of the entire Utah landings on D-Day. Additionally, ten US officers with BIGOT-level clearance had gone missing, Threatening *Neptune* with cancellation until all ten bodies were recovered. Security for *Overlord* demanded the entire Exercise Tiger disaster be covered up. Nevertheless, the Slapton Sands incident inspired several improvements. Radio frequencies were standardized, troops received better lifejacket training, and a rescue flotilla was added to pick up survivors afloat off the beaches. Admiral King transferred three LSTs from the Mediterranean to replace those lost during Tiger.

The final series of training exercises, the May 3–8 Exercise Fabius, was a grand dress rehearsal for the entire *Neptune* force, minus Moon's traumatized Force U. Directly commanded by Ramsay, Fabius was the largest amphibious exercise of the war and proved happily uneventful.

By May 30, some 1,100,146 US Army troops were stationed in the United Kingdom. Of these, 620,504 were Army Ground Force, while 459,511 belonged to Services of Supply or Headquarters. The final 20,131 were ETO staff or miscellaneous personnel. The USAAF contributed another 426,819 men. US naval forces in Britain came to 124,000 personnel, with 22,000 attached to naval bases, 15,000 to warships, and 87,000 to landing and beaching craft. Some 100,000 US naval personnel were lodged ashore, with another 25,000 living aboard ship.

The total US presence in the United Kingdom on May 30, 1944, reached 1,650,965 uniformed personnel, plus 5,297,306 tons of US supplies. The British Admiralty would eventually estimate that on D-Day there were 52,889 American and 112,824 British sailors afloat supporting the full *Neptune* operations.

COMBAT AND ANALYSIS

THE FLEET IN COMBAT
Launching *Overlord*, May 28–June 6, 1944

With such diverse ship speeds and ranges from sortie ports, each ship's time of departure varied from port to port and unit to unit. Moon's Force U would be first to sortie, as they were ported farthest from the Normandy destination. They departed from the West Country of England and would assemble south of the Isle of Wight. From the ports of south Devon, Force U's 865 ships began embarking troops and vehicles of the US 4th Infantry Division on June 1. Force U departed from Plymouth on June 3 and 4. Meanwhile, Hall's Force O also began loading troops and equipment at the Channel ports of Weymouth and Portland.

At 0500hrs on June 4, increasingly severe weather (driving rain, high seas, and a northwesterly Force 5 wind) caused SHAEF to delay the scheduled June 5 D-Day by 24 hours. To accommodate the tide, the new H-Hour was tentatively set for 0630hrs on June 6. All vessels already at sea were ordered to proceed to their emergency postponement ports, with troops miserably cooped up on their heaving vessels. However, convoy UA, carrying the US 4th Division to Utah, had to be discovered at sea by a Walrus plane and recalled via dropped canister message; the 150-ship convoy came about just 36nm from the Normandy coast.

The weather situation was serious. No postponement could be made to June 7, as many WNTF ships would have to refuel. A last-ditch postponement could be made to June 8, but unfavorable tides would then push the next invasion window to June 19. At this point, security issues might have demanded the entire invasion's cancellation. However, at 2115hrs on June 4, Eisenhower's meteorologist predicted a one- or two-day window of moderating wind and seas beginning early on June 6, admitting that June 8 and beyond were unpredictable. To meet the tentative June 6 D-Day, the fleet was forced to resume its sortie towards Normandy at 2300hrs on June 4, despite no final decision from SHAEF.

MINESWEPT CHANNELS TO OMAHA AND UTAH BEACHES

The final SHAEF weather conference at 0330hrs on June 5 was tentatively optimistic, and at 0415hrs Eisenhower simply announced: "OK. We'll go."

The Admiralty later estimated that 931 ships would cross the English Channel with the WNTF, and 1,796 ships with the ENTF. If one includes landing craft ferried aboard, and the ferry services' landing barges (which mostly did not cross), the figures come to 2,010 ships for the WNTF and 3,323 ships for the ENTF. The combined total of 5,333 ships is widely considered the largest invasion assault force ever assembled.

According to Rear Admiral Deyo:

"The great spring, wound so tightly, was now released; the vast energy loosed by that fateful signal began to travel down the length of the coil, slowly, almost imperceptibility, but gaining momentum. There was no turning back now; the unleashed energy must either turn into an inundating tidal wave to flood the shores of Normandy or shatter itself to pieces at the water's edge."[9]

The invasion begins

Force U's 16 Task Groups had loaded in nine different ports before assembling into 12 convoys to make the crossing, while Force O's 13 Task Groups had loaded in five different ports and assembled into five convoys. Usually, each convoy was made up of three or four sections of similar type or speed, most of which had to rendezvous at sea. Most LCTs, LCMs, and Rhino ferries either crossed the stormy Channel under their own power or were towed, with only LCVPs and LCAs typically being piggybacked aboard motherships. Although Force U had been badly disorganized by the postponement, Force O would cross with little problem. The battleships and cruisers of the WNTF sortied from Belfast, with most of their escorting destroyers joining them en route. Accompanying Hall's Force O to Omaha was the cruiser *Augusta*, the overall WNTF flagship carrying Rear Admiral Kirk and Lieutenant-General Bradley.

All five *Neptune* invasion forces, converging from the far reaches of the United Kingdom, were channeled into and through a previously swept circular zone south of the Isle of Wight officially designated Area Zebra but inevitably dubbed "Piccadilly Circus." Galley fires were put out at midnight, June 6, and all ships went to General Quarters and set watertight doors to the maximum setting of Condition Zebra.

"The mine," Ramsay had observed, "is our greatest obstacle to success." *Neptune* had assigned the minesweepers three sequential missions: to provide a safe passage for the assault forces to the transport area; to provide wider channels

9   *Naval Guns at Normandy* Naval Institute Press (2011)

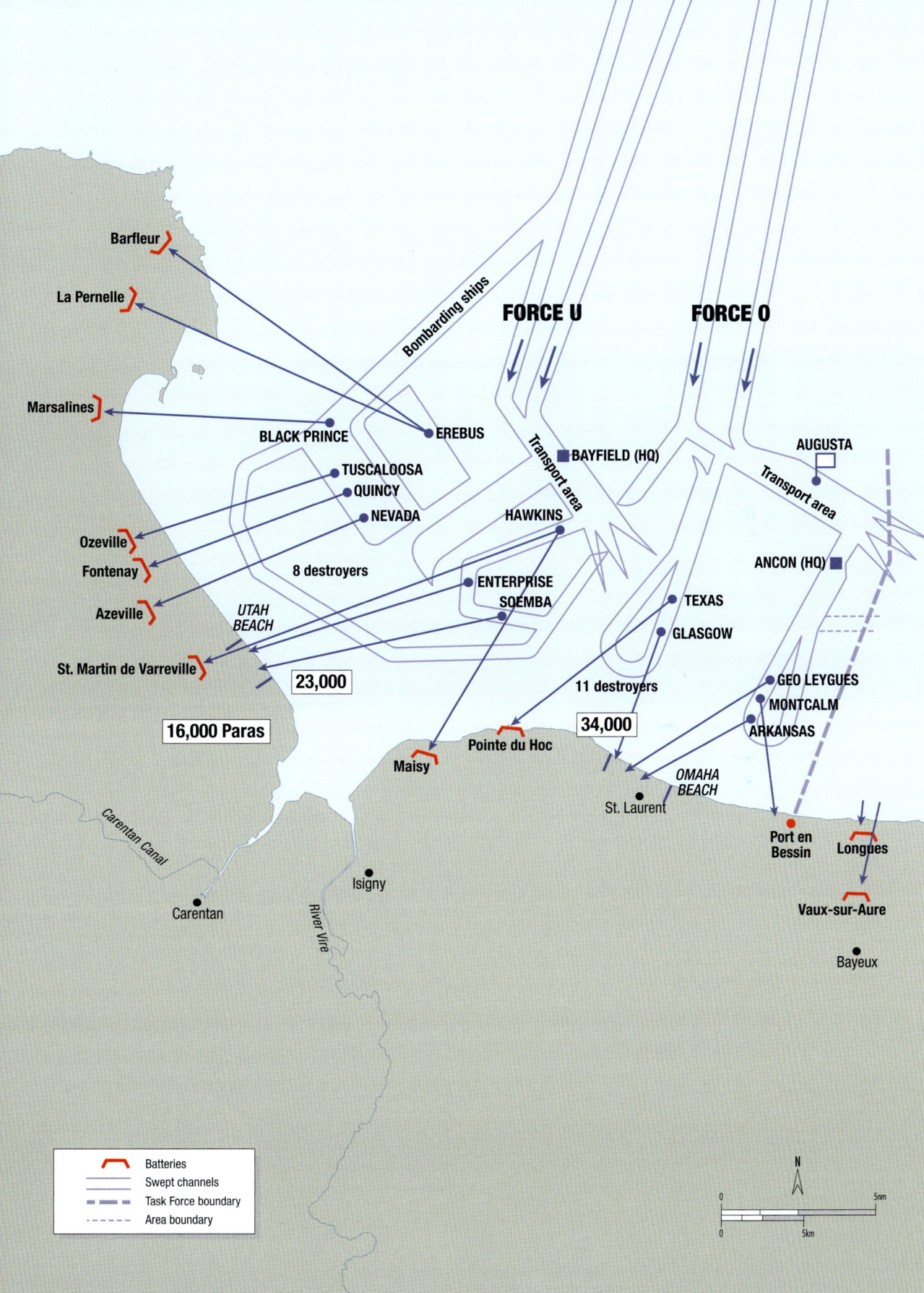

Barfleur

La Pernelle

Marsalines

BLACK PRINCE   EREBUS

TUSCALOOSA
QUINCY
NEVADA   HAWKINS

FORCE U   **FORCE O**

Bombarding ships

Transport area   AUGUSTA

BAYFIELD (HQ)   Transport area

ANCON (HQ)

Ozeville
Fontenay   ENTERPRISE
                        SOEMBA
Azeville
                UTAH   TEXAS
                BEACH   GLASGOW
St. Martin de Varreville
                                            GEO LEYGUES
          8 destroyers   MONTCALM
                                            ARKANSAS
                  23,000   11 destroyers
                                34,000
          16,000 Paras

                Maisy   Pointe du Hoc

                                OMAHA
                                BEACH
                        St. Laurent
                                        Port en   Longues
                                        Bessin
                                                Vaux-sur-Aure
Carentan Canal

                Isigny   Bayeux
River Vire

Carentan

Batteries
Swept channels
Task Force boundary
Area boundary

N

0   5nm

0   5km

to the beaches for shipping in the buildup; and finally, to sweep a channel, parallel to the beaches, which would be continuously broadened until it would form a safe anchorage and patrol area.

During the night of June 5–6, each minesweeper flotilla closed on the Normandy coast for four hours before reversing course along a parallel track. Small vessels followed behind the minesweepers, deploying floating red/green danbuoys to mark the swept channel edges. The minesweepers worked in groups of six, steaming in echelon the breadth of the desired channel.

However, on the evening of June 5, Mine Squadron 7's USS *Osprey* (AM-56) struck a mine that started fires and ripped open its forward engine room. At 1815hrs, *Osprey*'s skipper, Commander Henry Plander, ordered his ship abandoned. The burning *Osprey* sank shortly afterwards, having lost six men, the first casualties of *Overlord* .

Despite *Osprey*'s loss, at 0200hrs on June 6 the minesweepers began sweeping the transport area, approach areas, fire support area, and the boat lanes to within a mile of the French coast. The minesweepers would sweep two separate channels to each of Utah and Omaha – a fast 12-knot channel for attack transports and destroyers, and a slow 5-knot channel for landing craft. Once the Utah and Omaha channels had been swept and marked, the outbound minesweepers began sweeping the Utah and Omaha anchorage areas 11–12nm offshore, dedicated to the large attack transports.

At 2215hrs on June 5, some 925 C-47 transport planes of the US Ninth Air Force had begun launching from 25 airfields in western England. By 0130hrs on June 6, they would start dropping 13,000 paratroopers of the US 82nd and 101st Airborne Divisions at six designated drop zones behind Utah. Darkness, weather, and German anti-aircraft fire caused most drops to be badly scattered and 60 percent of their equipment to be lost. German defenders alerted LXXXIV Korps headquarters at 0215hrs on June 6, but Wehrmacht commanders appeared to believe the airborne landings were merely diversionary to the assumed main landings at the Pas-de-Calais.

A force of 36 U-boats based at Brest, L'Orient, Saint-Nazaire, and La Pallice had been assigned to counterattack any cross-Channel invasion fleet. An additional three German destroyers from Royan had also been forward-deployed to Brest. After German radar detected the invasion fleet, a Kriegsmarine alert was sounded at 0309hrs on June 6. Nevertheless, only 15 S-boats sortied, and these aborted because of the weather without ever sighting the *Neptune* invasion fleet. Indeed, the Kriegsmarine's

LCI(L) convoy crossing the English Channel after daybreak on June 6, 1944. Each is towing a barrage balloon to ward off low-altitude German aircraft (which ultimately never appeared). Visible are LCI(L)-56, LCI(L)-325, and LCI(L)-4. Many of these balloons would be cut loose after anchoring to avoid giving German coastal artillery obvious targets over the horizon. (NHHC 26-G-2333)

U-boats, destroyers, and S-boats all proved "no-shows" on D-Day. According to *Nevada*'s Captain Powell Rhea: "It was astounding, and certainly more than could be hoped for, to have been able to make the approach and anchor … [so close to] the enemy beaches completely unopposed."[10]

The four large Utah transports had dropped anchor in 17 fathoms (102ft) of water at 0229hrs. They were followed at 0251hrs by the 16 Omaha transports, which dropped anchor in two lines parallel to their own beach. Both Transport Areas were 12nm offshore. Arriving simultaneously with the transports were assault LSTs towing Rhino ferries and carrying the beach demolition team assault waves; the LSTs would not only dispatch their own assault waves but

10 *Amphibious Operations. The Invasion of Northern France. Western Naval Rask Force*. (US Fleet)

Mine Squadron 7's USS *Osprey* strikes a mine, evening of June 5 (overleaf)

USS *Osprey* (AM-56) was a Raven-class minesweeper built at the Norfolk Naval Yard, Virginia, and commissioned on December 16, 1940. She displaced 1,040 tons fully loaded and had a top speed of 18 knots. *Osprey*'s initial combat assignment after Pearl Harbor was patrol and escort duties in the Caribbean Sea area, although *Osprey* steamed across the Atlantic to engage in the surprise Operation *Torch* landings in North Africa on November 8, 1942. In particular, *Osprey* patrolled and guided the landing forces at Port Lyautey, Morocco, then performed its designed minesweeping duties off Casablanca. Upon completing this mission, *Osprey* returned to Norfolk, Virginia, for additional coastal patrol duties. Then on April 3, 1944, *Osprey* departed Virginia for England, where it was to be part of Mine Squadron 7 and assigned to the upcoming *Neptune* invasion of Nazi-occupied Normandy.

A total of 245 vessels, plus ten more in reserve, were required to sweep channels for all five British and American assault forces. The night of May 31–June 1 saw the clandestine laying of ten sonic underwater buoys to mark the starting points for the five assault groups; each assault group would receive two adjacent mineswept channels 400yds wide. They would be lit at 1-mile intervals by lighted danbuoys laid by Fairmile motor launches following immediately behind the minesweepers.

The morning of June 4 saw the Royal Navy's 14th Minecraft Flotilla, sweeping ahead of Force U, run into a concentration of mines just before they were scheduled to turn back. Despite worsening weather, Commander George Irvine (RNVR) stayed until the mines were believed to be swept up. However, HMS *Campbell* found itself nearly immobilized by floating naval mines, which had to be detonated in order to extricate the vessel.

Irvine's additional minesweeping attempt the following morning, June 5, was hampered by increasingly bad weather, and some mines were inevitably missed. The result was that later that evening, when Commander Henry Plander's Mine Squadron 7 was sweeping, minesweeper USS *Osprey* (AM-56) was struck by a mine near the location of HMS *Campbell*'s predicament the previous day. The explosion ripped open *Osprey*'s forward engine room and started fires. *Osprey*'s crew battled for an hour and 15 minutes to save the ship, but their efforts proved futile. At 1815hrs, Commander Henry Plander ordered the minesweeper to be abandoned. The burning *Osprey* sank shortly afterwards, having lost six men out of a crew of 105, the first casualties of *Overlord*. Most of *Osprey*'s survivors, including skipper Lieutenant-Commander Charles Henry Swimm (USNR), were picked up by Auk-class minesweeper USS *Chickadee* (AM-56), but six were rescued by PT boats PT-505 and PT-508.

The wreck of the *Osprey* currently lies on its side, having been discovered and dived on in 1997; *Osprey*'s recovered ship's bell was returned to US authorities in 2019.

The 1944 Dwight C. Shepler watercolor *Under the Enemy's Nose* portrays Canadian minesweepers of the Royal Canadian Navy Minesweeping Squadron 31 as they clear a bombardment lane towards Normandy during the night before D-Day. The Canadians are escorted by destroyers USS *Emmons* (DD-457) and USS *Doyle* (DD-494). Scattered moonlight is broken up by the nocturnal air attack against Pointe du Hoc. (NHHC 88-199-ES)

would loan LCVPs to the assault transports. Immediately behind the LSTs were DD tank-carrying LCTs, fire support craft, and LCMs. These were followed by LCTs which dropped anchor astern the LSTs. The final assault units to appear were the LCI(L) convoys, timed to arrive at H-Hour.

The respective Lines of Departure, where landing craft waves would circle, marshal, and finally depart for the beaches, were 18,000yds landwards from the two Transport Areas and 4,000yds from shore. The Line of Departure was delineated by an anchored line of Patrol Craft (PC). A mile farther back was a line of 110ft Subchasers (SC), which functioned as secondary control craft. Having been long overworked on escort duty, the PCs had only been allowed a few days before the invasion to train, while the SCs had arrived as the fleet was embarking and had received no training at all. Nevertheless, the subchasers would guide long columns of blacked-out LCTs through the mineswept channels towards the beaches, through long lines of floating danbuoys, with red lights glowing on the right and green lights to the left.

By 0400hrs, the minesweepers had cleared the fire support area close offshore. In his post-action report, Captain Powell Rhea of the battleship *Nevada* claimed the minesweepers "deserve the lion's share of the credit for the accomplishment of the mission … They not only swept and buoyed a remarkably clear and geographically accurate channel through the German mine fields, but did so at night, unescorted, in severe cross currents, in mine-infested waters, and in the face of possible enemy attack."[11]

11 *Amphibious Operations. Invasion of Northern France. Western Naval Task Force.* (US Fleet)

Water temperature was a hypothermia-inducing 55 degrees F, with swells running 3–6ft and rising. Landing craft bobbed heavily. Loading the assault troops into the landing craft would take about an hour; marshaling the loaded landing craft into their correct waves took another hour. The 12nm run-in to the beaches would then require two more hours to make the 0630hrs H-Hour, meaning troops would spend three or four hours in landing craft before making landfall, with the final 2 miles to be covered by a planned smokescreen. As an example, at 0230hrs, attack transport *Thomas Jefferson*, some 12nm off Omaha, began loading its assault troops into already-lowered LCVPs. By 0336hrs, *Thomas Jefferson* had finished loading its LCVPs, and the assault wave had successfully assembled and departed for shore by 0430hrs.

The high-latitude summer sun would provide 17 hours of daylight, with dawn at 0515hrs and sunrise at 0558hrs. Low water was at 0500hrs, yet Normandy's low, flat beaches create a fast-rising tide that consumes dry land quickly. On June 6, 1944, the Normandy tide would rise about 20ft between 0600hrs and 1100hrs, exceeding an inch per minute at 0900hrs. The US Army had wanted a high-tide landing to minimize the distance its troops had to run through the beach, whereas the US Navy had urged a low-tide landing to allow beach obstacles to be avoided and marked for destruction. The final 0630hrs compromise resulted in H-Hour occurring on a middling but rising tide, half an hour after sunrise. This meant the initial assault would beach 200yds short of the high-water mark, making infantry and engineers exceptionally vulnerable to raking German fire. The fast-rising tide would, however, assist the landing craft in extricating themselves.

Allied bombers began their pre-invasion bomb runs at 0520hrs. By sunrise, 1,333 RAF heavy bombers would drop 5,316 tons of bombs against German coastal artillery between Cherbourg and the Seine River mouth. Another 1,361 USAAF heavy bombers would unload 2,944 tons of ordnance on the invasion beaches; their bombs were fuzed for instantaneous detonation to avoid cratering the beaches and impeding Allied vehicles. However, the aerial preparation of the beaches would prove nearly useless.

Attack transport USS *Bayfield* (APA-33) loads landing craft off the Normandy coast on June 6, 1944. Commissioned in November 1943, *Bayfield* was the lead ship of the eponymous class and Rear Admiral Moon's Force U flagship, making it one of the most important vessels of the invasion. (NHHC 80-G-252391)

Utah Beach, June 6

The Force U flagship was the Coast Guard-manned attack transport USS *Bayfield* (APA-33). Riding *Bayfield* was Force U naval commander Rear Admiral Moon and his US Army counterpart, VII Corps commander Major-General J. Lawton Collins. The purpose of the Utah landings, on the far right (northwest) of the *Neptune* assault, was to cut off the Cotentin peninsula from Wehrmacht reinforcements. On D-Day, Collins' VII Corps Utah invasion force comprised the 8th, 22nd, and 12th Regimental Combat Teams of the US 4th Infantry Division.

The main H-Hour assault force at Utah comprised the US 4th Division's 8th RCT, plus the 70th Tank Battalion. They would be assisted by detachments from the 299th and 237th Combat Engineer Battalions. Utah only had two designated assault beaches: Beach Green on the northwest and Beach Red on the southeast; Beach Green was the far-right flank of the Allied landings at Normandy. The beaches at Utah were flat and featureless, making it difficult to get visual bearings from offshore. An unexpected cross-current would also confound landing craft navigation to the beach. However, being in the lee of the Cotentin peninsula protected Utah landings from the weather.

Defending Utah were two battalions of the static 709.Infanterie-Division, a coastal defense unit manning 28 coastal batteries, including 110 guns between 75mm and 170mm. In the hinterland behind Utah was the 91.Luftlande-Infanterie-Division.

At 0430hrs, Lieutenant-Colonel E. C. Dunn's US 4th Cavalry Group detachment of 132 troopers landed at the tiny but unoccupied Saint-Marcouf islets 4 miles off Utah. They were led in by four knife-armed swimmers to mark the beaches. The islets would be secured by 0530hrs, but mines laid there by the Germans would kill two and wound 17.

Deyo's Utah bombardment group, Bombardment Group C, comprised the battleship *Nevada*, monitor *Erebus*, cruisers *Hawkins*, *Quincy*, *Tuscaloosa*, *Black Prince*, and *Enterprise*, Dutch gunboat *Soemba*, eight destroyers, two destroyer-escorts, and two frigates. Separated into five support groups, this force was scheduled to open fire with batteries of 6in. and smaller at 0550hrs (H-40). Then, ten minutes before the landings, *Nevada* and *Quincy* were to open fire with their 14in. and 8in. guns respectively.

As dawn broke at 0505hrs, a German battery opened fire on the destroyers *Corry* and *Fitch*. Twenty minutes later, heavy German batteries began shooting at the spotted minesweepers just 3,500yds offshore. The cruiser HMS *Black Prince* immediately retaliated and was in turn fired upon by heavy artillery at Saint-Vaast-la-Hougue. Repeated requests to return fire were ignored by Deyo, but German artillery was soon landing near-misses against Deyo's cruisers. Deyo waited until all his ships had reached their assigned stations, then at 0536hrs announced: "Commence counter-battery bombardment!" Allied gunships immediately opened fire, some 25 minutes after the first German fire against

Force U but still 14 minutes before the bombardment's scheduled commencement.

Between 0605hrs and 0624hrs, some 269 US Ninth Air Force B-26 Marauders unloaded 525 tons of bombs against seven designated targets on Utah between les Dunes de Varreville and Beau Guillot. Many Marauders ducked to 3,500ft altitude to pierce the overcast. Roughly one-third of their ordnance fell between the low- and high-tide marks. At 0610hrs, Allied planes began laying smokescreens between Force U and the shoreline. The Utah close fire support group of 33 various craft now closed in on the beaches. Among them were 17 rocket-equipped LCT(R)s, which unloaded 5,000 5in. rockets against Utah while the initial assault waves were still 600yds short of the beach.

The Utah landings would be spearheaded by the 70th Tank Battalion, two of whose three medium tank companies comprised M4A1 Sherman DD tanks. The battalion's third medium tank company consisted of Shermans with wading trunks, while the battalion's single light tank company would land during the afternoon of D-Day.

Rear Admiral Morton L. Deyo, commander of the Utah Bombardment Group and later the Cherbourg bombardment force. Deyo retired in 1949 with the rank of vice-admiral. Shortly afterward, he wrote *Naval Guns at Normandy*, his gripping and poetic first-hand account of the Normandy bombardment. (80-G-231642)

Not including the swimming DD tanks, a total of 26 assault waves were scheduled to land at Utah between 0630hrs and 1230hrs. They would land within 10–20-minute increments of each other. The Line of Departure was 4,000yds from shore. Beach Green and Beach Red had each been assigned a primary and secondary control vessel. However, only three control vessels had departed the Utah Transport Area at 0455hrs, as the Beach Red secondary control vessel had fouled its propeller on a danbuoy. Then, around 0600hrs and still 7,000yds out, the Beach Red primary control vessel – already running 15 minutes late – hit a mine and sank. Shortly afterwards, an LCT following the Beach Green primary control vessel also struck a mine and foundered, causing many of the already behind-schedule landing craft to slow down. However, the Beach Green secondary control vessel took control of the situation, leading in the landing craft and signaling it would directly lead in all amphibious tanks. The plan dictated that the tank-bearing LCTs would launch their tanks 5,000yds from shore, but this was reduced to a mere 3,000yds to make up lost time.

Within 100yds of the beach, boat coxswains shouted down 25-yard intervals until their boats ran aground: "Ramp going down – Now!" While most landing craft beached at the water's edge, some hit sandbars or obstructions in deep water, making egress dangerous or even fatal. Additionally, deep, invisible runnels in the Normandy sand caused many men to step into seemingly shallow surf, only to suddenly plunge completely underwater. The same invisible runnels often caused discharging vehicles to suddenly tip forward and sink.

Utah's first wave of 20 LCVPs – ten each for Beach Green and Beach Red – touched down exactly at H-Hour, 0630hrs. These first 600 troops (F and E Companies of 2nd Battalion/8th Infantry) waded 100yds to dry land, coming under no fire. A strong current and a desire to avoid swamping the DD tanks meant that the first landing waves had been pushed 2,000yds southeast of the planned landing site, which proved highly fortuitous. The second wave of 16 LCVPs, carrying G and H Companies of the 3/8th Infantry, plus 11 Underwater Demolition Teams, landed at 0635hrs. By 0800hrs, they would neutralize the relatively sparse beach obstacles ashore, clearing 700yds of beach.

Following this wave of LCVPs were eight late-arriving LCTs carrying 32 M4A1 DD tanks of B Company, 70th Tank Battalion, which landed at 0640hrs. One LCT hit a mine and sank, losing four tanks. Five minutes later came four LCTs with eight gun and eight dozer tanks from C Company, 70th Tank Battalion. The next wave followed two minutes later, carrying the 237th and 299th Engineer Combat Battalions, which were assigned to beach obstacle clearance. However, two LCTs carrying the engineers' dozer tanks were sunk, and an LCM filled with engineers was hit by German artillery fire just as it dropped its ramp on Beach Green. Nevertheless, the first five waves each for Utah Green and Utah Red had landed on time, although in the wrong place. Brigadier-General Teddy Roosevelt, Jr, landing with the first wave, convinced the Utah beachmaster to simply designate this the new Utah Beach, an inspired decision.

Although destroyers depend on high speed and maneuverability for defense, at Normandy they would be tied close to shore in a near-stationary, close-range slugfest with fortified German artillery batteries. The battleships and cruisers would be confined to deeper water much farther away. All would be restricted to maneuvering only in swept areas.

Before the landings, the plane laying smoke for the destroyer USS *Corry* (DD-463) was shot down, leaving *Corry* exposed. At 0633hrs, just as the assault landed, *Corry* was hit by concentrated German artillery fire. Compelled to maneuver away from subsequent German salvos, it steamed straight into a German naval mine, which exploded into the engine room and broke its keel. With its rudder jammed, the ship was unable to maneuver, and another German shell detonated its 40mm magazine.

Aged battleship USS *Nevada* (BB-36) unleashes its 14in. guns against Utah targets on the morning of June 6, 1944. *Nevada* had been the only battleship to get underway during the Pearl Harbor attack. A California radioman, witnessing the defiant escape attempt, described the event: "I had never seen anything so gallant. Some of us were crying unashamed tears. [Ultimately] ... the sortie of the *Nevada* failed. It remains the most magnificent heart-stopping failure I have ever seen." (US Navy)[12]

12 *Battleship Sailor*, Theodore Mason,. Naval Institute Press (2013)

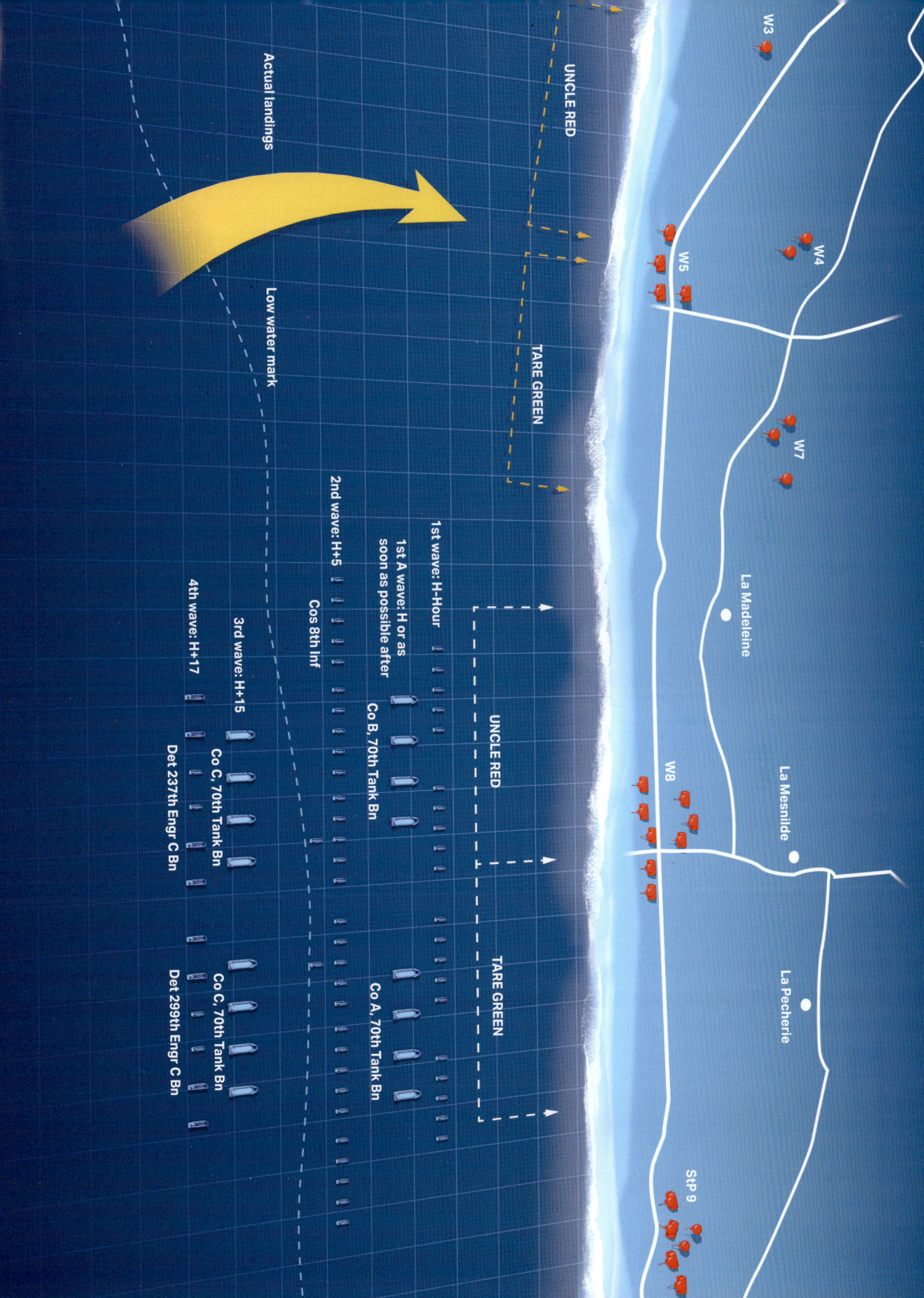

At 0640hrs, *Corry*'s skipper, Lieutenant-Commander G. D. Hoffman, gave the order to abandon ship. By 0729hrs, *Corry* had settled on the shallow bottom 3 miles offshore, with much of its superstructure still breaking the surface. *Corry* had suffered 22 killed and 33 wounded.

Tuscaloosa, *Nevada*, *Quincy*, *Hobson*, and *Fitch* all began slinging shells into the battery that had helped sink *Corry*; the stricken destroyer's men could only be rescued after the German artillery had been taken out. Most of *Corry*'s crew were picked up by the destroyer *Fitch*, which then departed the beach for the Transport Area to transfer *Corry*'s wounded. The destroyer *Gherardi* promptly took up *Fitch*'s vacated station, while destroyer *Butler* arrived to replace *Corry*, despite the danger of colliding with *Corry*'s wreckage in the cramped maneuvering space.

By midmorning, Force U had already lost one destroyer, one patrol craft, three LCTs, and an LCF to naval mines. Despite the otherwise successful landings, Moon shortly announced to VII Corps commander Major-General Collins that he intended to suspend the Utah landings until his minesweepers could fully clear the shallows. A shocked Collins persuaded Moon to continue the landings.

With the help of air spotting, the battleship *Nevada*, monitor *Erebus*, heavy cruisers *Tuscaloosa* and *Quincy*, and light cruiser *Black Prince* continued hammering heavy enemy batteries north of Utah near Saint-Vaast-la-Hougue until 0720hrs. Meanwhile, farther inshore, light cruiser *Enterprise* and the destroyers did the same. Afterwards, the bombardment ships would either hit targets of opportunity or respond to requests from the 18 landed fire control parties.

German batteries were typically active until they received heavy return fire from the Allied gunships, then they would fall silent. However, it was extremely difficult for airborne or seaborne observers to determine whether a silenced German battery had in fact been destroyed. Lacking the ammunition to waste on guns that were no longer shooting, Allied vessels would move on to other targets. After an hour or more, the previously silenced German batteries would roar to life again, requiring Allied gunships to again retaliate. Deyo admitted this was "a tedious and trying procedure," although "as long as their fire is directed at our ships and away from the troops, we have no complaint. That is what we are there for."[13]

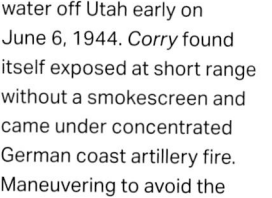

Destroyer USS *Corry* (DD-463) sinks in the shallow water off Utah early on June 6, 1944. *Corry* found itself exposed at short range without a smokescreen and came under concentrated German coast artillery fire. Maneuvering to avoid the German salvos, it steamed into a naval mine which broke its back. (US Navy)

---

13 *Naval Guns at Normandy*, Vice Admiral Morton L. Deyo

Around 1200hrs, German batteries near Carentan began bombarding the improvised Utah beaches. The heavy cruiser HMS *Hawkins*, Dutch gunboat *Soemba*, and destroyer USS *Herndon* were assigned to take them out. HMS *Enterprise* would receive six total fire support calls from its forward spotter. It responded with 145 6in. rounds against German fortifications northeast of Pouppeville, while HMS *Black Prince* "fired rapidly with her 5.25-inch guns on several troublesome targets."

The US 82nd and 101st Airborne Division landings behind Utah Beach had scattered so badly that, despite not fully accomplishing their objectives, they had thoroughly bewildered the German defenses. Accompanying the six US paratrooper regiments were nine jump-qualified spotters attached to the 101st Airborne Division (one spotter to each battalion). By 1120hrs, radio contact had been successfully established with the heavy cruiser *Quincy*. Throughout June 6, *Quincy* would successfully respond to eight separate calls for naval fire support from the 101st Airborne. All eight missions were targeted at reported concentrations of German troops massing on the Carentan–Sainte-Mère-Église highway. In between, *Quincy* targeted harassing Cotentin batteries to the right of Utah.

Nevada also provided major fire support to the US paratroopers behind Utah, obliterating a group of panzers and German field artillery and thereby persuading the Germans to transfer their marshaling area elsewhere. By nightfall, *Nevada* would unload 337 shells from its 14in. guns and another 2,693 rounds from its 5in. battery.

For its part, the heavy cruiser *Tuscaloosa* would expend 487 8in. and 115 5in. shells on D-Day in 16 separate shoots, most aimed deep inland. In turn, *Tuscaloosa* would be targeted three times by German batteries, but no enemy shell landed within 300yds of it.

Transport *Empire Gauntlet* had fully unloaded by 0830hrs, followed by *Dickman* and *Barnett* by 1243hrs; all three were back in Portland by late evening. At 1400hrs, Major-General Barton had established his 4th Division headquarters ashore. By 1800hrs, Force U had successfully landed 21,328

World War I-era British monitor HMS *Erebus* seen in early 1944. *Erebus'* two 15in. guns in a single turret were the largest guns in the Western Naval Task Force. Commissioned in September 1916, *Erebus* was a specialized gunship intended for close gunfire support in shallow waters. (Public Domain)

USS LST-73 approaches Normandy beaches off Utah on June 6, 1944. LST-73 is carrying troops and equipment of the 8th Regiment, 4th Infantry Division. LST-73 was a member of the original LST-1 class, of which 390 were ultimately built. (NHHC SC 190462)

troops, 1,742 vehicles, and 1,695 tons of supplies at Utah and effectively thrown the German defenders off the beach. Cool leadership ashore had prevented the 1-mile navigation error from developing into an operational disaster. Except for a single field artillery battalion, the US 4th Infantry Division was entirely ashore by evening, having suffered only 197 casualties assaulting Utah. However, another 700 men had been lost from the US 70th Tank Battalion, engineer units, and vessels and craft sunk during the assault. Additionally, the US 82nd and 101st Airborne Divisions had landed about 14,000 troops behind Utah via parachute and glider, suffering 2,500 casualties. US VII Corps commander Collins elected to spend the night of June 6–7 aboard the *Bayfield* because it allowed him much superior communications. The Force U commander, Rear Admiral Moon, reported that there was "little to write about the assault" as Utah had gone "essentially according to plan."

Omaha Beach, June 6

Carrying the initial Omaha assault force of 34,000 men and 3,300 vehicles were seven transports, eight LSIs, 24 LSTs, 33 LCI(L)s, 36 LCM(3)s, 147 LCTs, and 33 other craft. The Omaha bombardment, gunfire support, and escort elements comprised two battleships, three cruisers, 12 destroyers, and 105 other ships. Omaha minesweeping and auxiliary duties entailed 33 minesweepers and 585 additional craft.

The Force O flagship was the command transport USS *Ancon* (AGC-4). Aboard *Ancon* was Force O naval commander Rear Admiral Hall, US V Corps commander Major-General L. T. Gerow, and US 1st Infantry Division commander Major-General Clarence Huebner. Omaha's initial dawn assault would land the 1st Infantry Division's 16th RCT on the east (left) and the US 29th Infantry Division's 116th RCT and most of the US Provisional Ranger Group (two battalions) on the west (right). By afternoon, follow-up waves would land the rest of 1st Division (18th and 26th RCTs) and 29th

Division (115th and 175th RCTs) behind their respective assault RCTs. But unlike the Utah landings, Omaha would be battered by heavy seas.

As the Normandy shore turns east from the Cotentin peninsula, the coast turns into high cliffs followed by steep sandy bluffs. A narrow pebbly shore wraps the base of the westerly cliffs, but wide, sandy beaches front the subsequent 3 miles of bluffs. These 3 miles were Omaha Beach. The steep bluffs fronting Omaha and high cliffs flanking it on either side made excellent defensive positions for German artillery and machine guns to enfilade the low, 300yd-wide beach in front of them. Additionally, the 150ft bluffs backing Omaha were too steep even for tracked vehicles, meaning the only way off Omaha and inland were four wooded ravines or "draws," of which only two could support tracked vehicles. Finally, 3 miles west of Omaha was Pointe du Hoc, where US intelligence had registered six casemated heavy guns, dubbed "the most dangerous battery in France."

Omaha's Bombardment Force C, commanded by Rear Admiral Carleton F. Bryant, steams into line on the morning of June 6, 1944. They are led by the battleship *Texas*, followed by cruiser *Glasgow*, battleship *Arkansas*, and then the French cruisers *Montcalm* and *Georges Leygues*. (IWM A 23923)

Because of Omaha's foreboding terrain, a US Army study had determined that a single defending Wehrmacht regiment would inflict heavy casualties on the assault force, while a full division would be virtually unassailable. However, US intelligence believed only a single understrength and largely immobile regiment defended Omaha. But in fact, since late March 1944, Omaha had been reinforced by the full 352.Infanterie. Division, a young, well-trained, and well-armed front-line unit.

Many concealed gun emplacements capable of enfilading the entire beach had been dug directly into the Omaha bluffs; guns that had gone entirely unnoticed by Allied photoreconnaissance analysts and would prove a nasty surprise to the American assault. Omaha additionally boasted 3,700 beach obstacles, making its defenses the densest of *Neptune*'s five landing sectors. Indeed, Force O commander Hall had unsuccessfully urged an 0400hrs H-Hour to allow the demolition teams an additional two-and-a-half hours to clear underwater obstacles; Omaha's June 6 tidal range would be a foreboding 22ft in the morning and 23ft in the afternoon. Nevertheless, during the tense weather of June 2, Hall had told a friend: "I do not expect to be repulsed on any beach." Yet Omaha was the only Normandy assault that appeared close to failing entirely and was the only sector that Allied commanders seriously considered evacuating. That neither event transpired attests partly to the steadfast Hall, who simply refused to entertain Omaha's failure.

Omaha Beach seen in July 2011, just over 67 years after the battle. Some additional development encroaches on the bluffs, and the shingle beach section was entirely removed by Allied engineers in the immediate aftermath of D-Day, but otherwise the terrain holds up well to what it was in June 1944. Omaha's qualities as a natural defensive fire sack are painfully apparent. (Credit to Anton Bielousov under CC BY-SA 3.0 license)

Rear Admiral C. F. Bryant's Omaha Bombardment Group (Force A) would commence naval gunfire at 0550hrs and cease at 0627hrs, three minutes before H-Hour. The destroyers would deploy 5,000–7,000yds off Omaha to provide close-in pre-landing bombardment. The battleships and cruisers, stationed 18,000yds out, would simply fire over the destroyers.

The battleship *Texas*, cruiser *Glasgow*, and five destroyers would provide naval gunfire support for the western and central landing zones at Omaha, including Pointe du Hoc. At 0550hrs, the *Texas* opened fire with its secondary battery against German strongpoints along the beach exit to Vierville. It was shortly joined by the destroyer *McCook*, LCG-424, LCT-464, and PC-568. Yet despite 190 5in. rounds from *Texas* alone, the bombardment failed to achieve its objectives.

Bombardment ships assigned to eastern Omaha were the battleship *Arkansas* and the two French light cruisers *Georges Leygues* and *Montcalm*. They were joined by six DesRon-18 destroyers assigned to provide close fire support. From west to east, *Tanatside*, *Emmons*, *Baldwin*, and *Harding* were responsible for Beaches Easy Red to Fox Green; *Doyle* was responsible for the cliff overlooking the Fox Red beach exit; and *Melbreak* would target the road junction at the village of Sainte-Honorine. Each destroyer's station was assigned so that it would have a clear field of fire to its target, without shooting across an adjacent destroyer's zone.

At 0530hrs, a German battery opened on the battleship *Arkansas*. Simultaneously, the French light cruiser *Montcalm* returned fire from its anchorage 7,500yds offshore. "You may well imagine," Contre-Amiral Robert Jaujard later confessed, "what emotion was aroused when we were ordered to bombard our homeland! But it was part of the price we had to pay for defeat in 1940."[14]

The scheduled naval bombardment of Omaha began at 0550hrs and lasted for 35 minutes. The destroyers *Satterlee*, *McCook*, *Carmick*, and *Baldwin*, along with LCT-520, were all shot at, to no avail. Nor did Force O suffer any initial damage to mines. At 0600hrs, 480 B-24 heavy bombers of the US VIII Bomber Command were tasked to drop 1,285 tons of bombs on 13 Omaha Beach strongpoints. Ordnance was instantaneously fuzed to avoid cratering the beach and slowing the advance. However, the night before, VIII Bomber Command

14 *The Invasion of France and Germany* Naval Institute Press (2011)

had ordered bombs to be dropped 30 seconds late to avoid hitting landing craft, because planners anticipated low overcast at H-Hour. Not a single bomb would thus land near the Omaha beaches, with some hitting as far as 3 miles inland. To the west, 18 US Ninth Air Force medium bombers were to hit batteries infesting Pointe du Hoc. Another 18 medium bombers would simultaneously strike Maisy, with Maisy's and Gefosse-Fontenay's gun positions targeted by two squadrons of fighter-bombers.

Battleship USS *Arkansas* and an LCT at Omaha on June 6, 1944. *Arkansas* was the oldest battleship at Normandy, having been commissioned in 1912 and sporting a dozen 12in. guns. So old was *Arkansas* that its sistership *Wyoming* had been demilitarized before the war and converted into an antiaircraft training ship, a role *Wyoming* performed throughout World War II. (Australian War Memorial Photo No. P02018.287)

Commander W. J. Marshall, DesDiv-36 commander, reported: "At 0617 (H minus 13 minutes) LCT(R)s commenced firing rockets, drenching the area just inland from the beaches. Fire from this beach was temporarily silenced and the entire area covered with heavy smoke and dust."[15] Five LCG(L)s, armed with two 47mm guns, would accompany Omaha's opening assault wave. As planned, the naval bombardment would crescendo and then trail off a few minutes before Omaha's 0630hrs H-Hour.

Western Omaha was to be assaulted by Captain W. O. Bailey's Assault Group O-2, which would land the US 29th Division's 116th RCT. The primary transports for the assault wave were US attack transports *Charles Carroll* and *Thomas Jefferson* plus British LSI(L) *Empire Javelin*. The 116th RCT's A, G, and F Companies were to land at Beaches Dog Green, Dog White, and Dog Red respectively, while E Company would land on Beach Easy Green. These units would seize two beach exits, one leading to Saint-Laurent and the other to Vierville-sur-Mer. Just west of Dog Green was rugged Beach Charlie, which was assigned a single Ranger company.

Commander S. H. Dennis' Assault Group O-4 was an entirely Royal Navy affair. Its six LSI transports would land the US 2nd and 5th Ranger Battalions at Pointe du Hoc and Beach Dog Green in Omaha's central sector. Assault Group O-4 additionally embarked US V Corps' floating reserve, the 115th RCT of the US 29th Division. The most formidable objective of the entire *Neptune* landings was Pointe du Hoc, an abrupt, 117ft promontory projecting seawards and rising vertically from a narrow shingle beach. Atop Pointe du Hoc, the Germans had mounted a casemated six-gun 155mm battery that had a range of 25,000yds and enfiladed both beaches. Eliminating this critical strongpoint would require Assault Group O-4's 2nd Ranger Battalion "to land on a rough shingle beach covered by several machine-gun positions, then to scale an almost perpendicular cliff almost as high as a ten-story building and

---

15 *Destroyers at Normandy* Naval, Historical Foundation (1994)

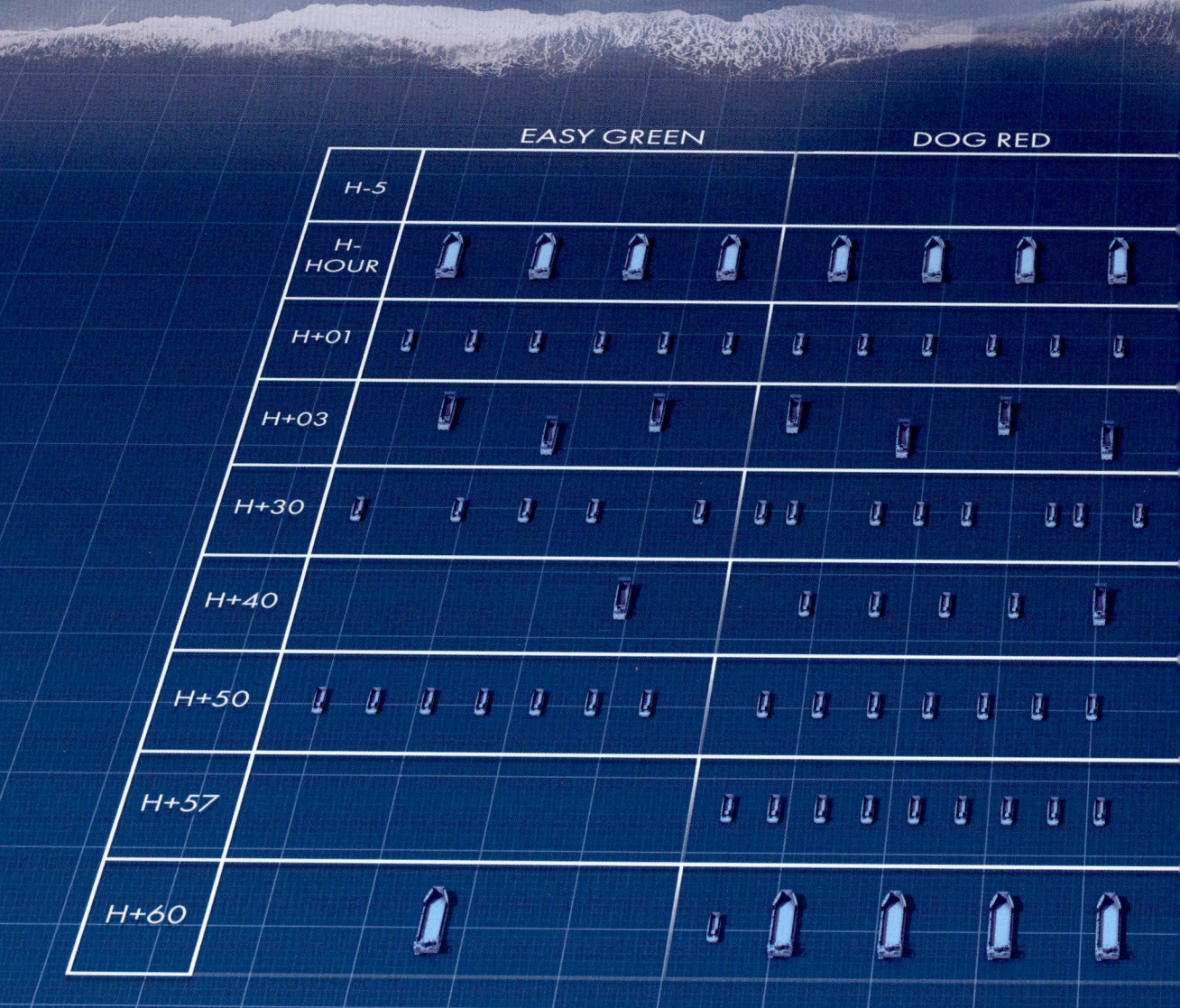

	EASY GREEN				DOG RED			
H-5								
H-HOUR	⛵	⛵	⛵	⛵	⛵	⛵	⛵	⛵
H+01	▯ ▯ ▯ ▯ ▯ ▯				▯ ▯ ▯ ▯ ▯ ▯			
H+03	▯	▯	▯		▯ ▯		▯	▯
H+30	▯	▯ ▯ ▯		▯	▯▯ ▯ ▯		▯▯	▯
H+40			▯		▯	▯	▯	▯
H+50	▯ ▯ ▯ ▯ ▯ ▯				▯ ▯ ▯ ▯ ▯			
H+57					▯ ▯ ▯ ▯ ▯ ▯ ▯ ▯			
H+60	⛵			⛵	⛵ ⛵	⛵	⛵	

THE US 116TH RCT LANDINGS AT OMAHA: THE FIRST HOUR OF D-DAY

At H-5, that is five minutes before H-Hour, two companies of Sherman DD tanks from the US 743rd Tank Battalion were to touch down at Omaha. Company C would land at Beach Dog White, and Company B would land immediately to the right at Dog Green. Each company wielded 16 tanks, for a combined total of 32 Sherman DD tanks spearheading the invasion. At H-Hour, the DD tanks would be followed by eight LCTs carrying Sherman tanks of the 743rd Tank Battalion's Company A. These would land to the left of the DD tanks, at beaches Easy Green and Dog Red. These tanks were expected to provide immediate fire support to the oncoming first wave.

One minute later, at H+1, came the first infantry, carried by 24 LCVPs and LCAs spread out with six landing craft per beach. These were from Companies E, F, G, and A. Thirteen LCMs carrying engineers would arrive two minutes later, at H+3, accompanied by two LCAs carrying troops from Company C, 2nd Ranger Battalion. The engineers would help eliminate beach obstacles for following waves and were ostensibly supported by the previously landed infantry and tanks.

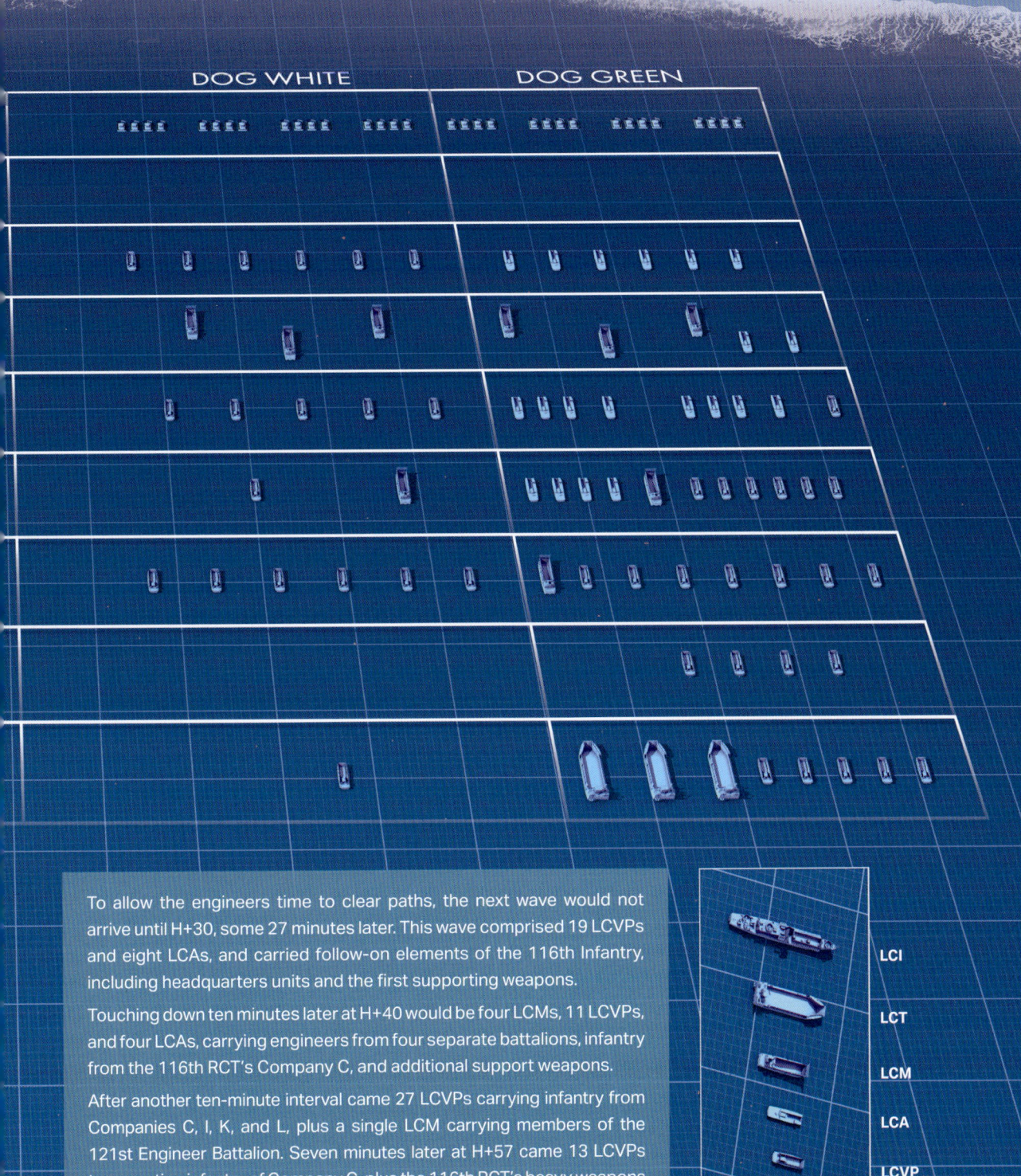

DOG WHITE   DOG GREEN

To allow the engineers time to clear paths, the next wave would not arrive until H+30, some 27 minutes later. This wave comprised 19 LCVPs and eight LCAs, and carried follow-on elements of the 116th Infantry, including headquarters units and the first supporting weapons.

Touching down ten minutes later at H+40 would be four LCMs, 11 LCVPs, and four LCAs, carrying engineers from four separate battalions, infantry from the 116th RCT's Company C, and additional support weapons.

After another ten-minute interval came 27 LCVPs carrying infantry from Companies C, I, K, and L, plus a single LCM carrying members of the 121st Engineer Battalion. Seven minutes later at H+57 came 13 LCVPs transporting infantry of Company C, plus the 116th RCT's heavy weapons battalion and its 3rd Battalion's headquarters company. Finally at H+60 came eight LCTs, five LCAs, and two LCVPs carrying engineers, Rangers, and the 116th RCT's headquarters company.

LCI

LCT

LCM

LCA

LCVP

DUKW

DD M4

LCVPs from attack transport *Samuel Chase* churn towards a foreboding Omaha Beach on the morning of June 6, 1944. Relatively little wreckage is apparent near the shore or on the beach, indicating this official US Coast Guard photograph may have been depicting one of the initial assault waves. (NARA 26-G-2337)

capture the battery."[16] The destroyer USS *Satterlee* (DD-626) and escort destroyer HMS *Talybont* would provide direct gunfire support at Pointe du Hoc. As added insurance to the Ranger assault, the battleship *Texas* slung 176 tons of 14in. shells at Pointe du Hoc prior to H-Hour. It was joined by British light cruiser *Glasgow*.

However, the nine LCAs carrying the 2nd Ranger Battalion landed at Pointe du Hoc 35 minutes late, at 0705hrs. This gave the German defenses a full 40 minutes to recover after the rigidly scheduled naval bombardment had ceased at 0625hrs. According to *Texas'* captain: "Had this vessel, or the inshore destroyers, known the plight of the Rangers at H-hour, fire could have been continued, keeping the enemy down until the Rangers could scale the cliff and over-run the area."[17] As *Satterlee's* skipper bitterly explained: "Naval gunfire support should conform to the movement of the landing boats rather than adhere to a predetermined time schedule." Even Hall's own intelligence officer had scoffed at the plan to assault Pointe du Hoc: "It can't be done. Three old women with brooms could keep the Rangers from climbing that cliff."

Nevertheless, the Rangers, armed with rocket-propelled grapnels, began pulling themselves up the cliff while under German small-arms fire. They were assisted by an unplanned 40ft-high mound of spoil – the result of *Texas* 14in. shells that had collapsed a section of cliff. When the surviving Rangers finally succeeded in scaling the precipice, they discovered the casemates empty. Further reconnaissance revealed that four guns had been removed and redeployed in a hedge lane a mile to the south. Within hours, *Texas* would bombard these guns and knock them out with the assistance of air spotting. The destroyer *Harding* (DD-625) would eventually land a whaleboat of naval infantry to relieve Rangers from guarding German prisoners.

Captain E. H. Fritzsche's Assault Group O-1, composed primarily of attack transports *Samuel Chase* and *Henrico*, and the British LSI(L) *Empire Anvil*, would land the US 1st Division's 16th RCT on the eastern Omaha beaches. The 16th RCT's E and F Companies would land at Beach Easy Red, while I and L Companies assaulted Beach Fox Green. They would secure eastern Omaha's three beach exits leading to Saint-Laurent, Colleville, and Cabourg. Following astern of Fritzsche's Assault Group O-1 was Captain L. B. Schulten's Assault

16 *The Invasion of France and Germany* Naval Institute Press (2011)
17 *Amphibious Operations. Invasion of Northern France. Western Naval Task Force.* (US Fleet)

Group O-3, centered around transports *Anne Arundel*, *Dorothea L. Dix*, and *Thurston*. Schulten's O-3 would land the 18th RCT following the 16th RCT's initial assault waves.

Leading the full Omaha assault were the 741st and 743rd Tank Battalions, which would provide a combined 112 amphibious M4A1 Sherman tanks ahead of the 16th and 116th RCTs respectively. Of these, 64 were DD tanks carried by two groups of eight LCTs each, while the remaining 48 Shermans were wading tanks. Rear Admiral Hall and the US Army corps and divisional commanders had agreed to launch the DDs from the LCTs between 1,000 and 6,000yds out if sea conditions allowed; if not, the LCTs were authorized to land directly on the beach. The decision would be made by the senior officer aboard each LCT, regardless of military branch.

The eastern LCT group carrying the 741st Tank Battalion was commanded by a US Army captain. Although the morning's 6ft waves at Omaha far exceeded the DD tanks' safety margins, the Army captain ordered his DD tanks launched from 5,000yds. Immediately swamped by high waves, almost all began to founder and sink. However, after seeing its first tank roll off and sink, LCT-600 retracted its ramp and ran all the way in. Of the 29 DD tanks that did try to swim into Omaha, just two made it, resulting in 33 drowned tank crewmen. However, Lieutenant D. L. Rockwell (USNR), commanding the western LCT group, landed the entire 743rd Tank Battalion directly ashore.

The LCVPs of the first official wave landed at 0631hrs, most grounding 50–100yds offshore. This first Omaha wave comprised 1,450 troops in eight assault companies, plus GAT teams. German machine-gun fire was already hammering the LCVPs before their bow ramps dropped. Men who avoided being immediately shot often fell into water up to their necks as they struggled forward through the bullet-whipped surf. Many leapt over the sides and sank out of sight, weighed down by their unusually heavy assault kit. Those who survived the desperate trudge to shore had another 200yds of beach to cross before reaching even the barest safety of the shingle or seawall. Slight cover was provided by the dust and smoking grass fires churned up by the bombardment.

The larger, second assault wave reached Omaha at 0700hrs, but the shattered and virtually paralyzed survivors of the first wave were unable to provide any covering fire. This second wave now faced the same enemy firepower and inadequately cleared channels as before, but with the added disadvantage of having to plow through the congested first wave wreckage in front of them.

Into the Jaws of Death by Coast Guardsman Robert F. Sargent is arguably the most famous and evocative photograph from the initial D-Day assault. It depicts a Coast Guard-manned LCVP from *Samuel Chase* debarking troops of A Company, 16th Infantry, 1st Infantry Division onto the Fox Green section of Omaha Beach early on June 6, 1944. (US Coast Guard)

Then at 0830hrs, the Omaha LCI(L)s reached the traffic-jammed beach. An LCI(L) training manual had happily declared: "Hedgehogs, stakes, or tetrahedra will not prevent your beaching provided you go flat out. Your craft will crunch over them, bend them and squash them into the sand and the damage to your outer bottom can be accepted. So drive on." A few LCI(L) crews risked following this advice. Provided no mines were attached to the beach obstructions, the manual proved correct.

The hour of crisis

The fierce German defense had inflicted 70 percent casualties on the 16 GAT demolition teams assigned to Omaha. Of the teams' 16 assigned dozer tanks, only six had made it ashore, and all but one had been quickly knocked out. Consequently, only five of 16 planned 50-yard-wide channels had been cleared through the beach obstacles by 0800hrs, when the tide began to rise. Meanwhile, landed vehicles were unable to fight their way off the beach and inland. First vehicles and then landing craft began backing up, throwing Omaha into chaos. Arriving landing craft milled aimlessly back and forth, desperately trying to find marked channels or any open lane at all. In their ad hoc attempts to reach shore, many boats collided, with one participant being reminded of bumper cars. The traffic-snarled Omaha beaches increasingly became a shooting gallery for the German defenders. Then, just as the LCI(L) wave arrived at 0830hrs, the Omaha beachmaster informed Hall that "they were stopping the advance of follow-up waves." Kirk later admitted to being "worried, very much worried about Omaha."[18]

18 *Neptune,* Craig Symonds (2016)

The Tough Beach, a 1944 watercolor by Dwight C. Shepler, depicts an LCI forcing its way ashore against a heavily fortified and obstructed Omaha Beach. Omaha was heavily studded with beach and underwater obstacles, mines, and German fortified positions and pillboxes. (NHHC 88-199-EU)

DesRon-18's orders had been to engage in the pre-landing bombardment and then pull away from the landing beaches immediately before H-Hour, to clear space for the assault waves. However, it was soon obvious that the Omaha landings were not going according to plan. Without orders, individual destroyers had begun closing on Omaha around 0800hrs to fire on any targets that presented themselves. Thirty minutes later, Hall formalized the destroyers' initiative and ordered them to "maintain as heavy a fire on beach target[s] as possible."

The destroyers now closed to within 1,000yds of the beach. Maneuvering within a very restricted area and fighting strong currents and mediocre visibility, the destroyers had to simultaneously avoid running aground, colliding with each other, and running over landing craft and other wreckage, all while keeping their batteries unmasked and providing accurate fire against German targets.

At 0830hrs, the destroyer *Carmick* observed "a group of tanks … having difficulty … A silent cooperation was established wherein they fired at a target on the bluff above them and we then fired several salvos at the same spot. They then shifted fire further along the bluff and we used their bursts again as a point of aim. This continued as they slowly advanced along the breakwater."

The destroyer *Frankford*, the DesRon-18 flagship, closed in on Omaha just before 0900hrs: "It was becoming clear to the destroyer captains that the landings were not going as planned." Aboard *Frankford*, Captain Sanders now ordered all destroyers to move as close to the beach as possible and begin delivering support gunfire. Sanders was seconded by Rear Admiral Bryant, who at 0950hrs radioed his gunships: "Get on them, men! Get on them! They are

Texas (BB-35) supporting the Rangers at Pointe du Hoc

(overleaf)

The US Rangers who landed at Pointe du Hoc on the morning of June 6 had been unable to fully secure their position, and by the morning of June 7 were engaged in an intense firefight, suffering effective counterattacks from German infantry. The Rangers' ability to hold the promontory at all, and not be driven straight back into the sea, came into question.

At 1130hrs, the *Texas* received a message from destroyer USS *Harding* (DD-625) that the Ranger force at Pointe du Hoc was in serious difficulty and needed small arms, ammunition, and food, and that there were many wounded at the base of the Pointe du Hoc cliff who were in urgent need of medical attention. The Rangers also requested reinforcements, but none were immediately available.

In response, *Texas* commandeered two LCVPs and loaded them with food, 0.30-caliber ammunition, and water and dispatched them to the beach below Pointe du Hoc. *Texas* can be seen here a few miles off Pointe du Hoc. The 573ft-long battleship *Texas*, with its beam of 95ft, easily dwarfs the 33ft-long, 10ft-wide LCVPs it is loading.

That afternoon, the two LCVPs returned to *Texas* with 35 wounded Rangers, one dead Coast Guardsman, and 27 prisoners-of-war (20 Germans, four Italians, and three French). The LCVPs arrived back at *Texas* around 1930hrs, and for the next ten hours *Texas*' entire medical staff went to work on the injured personnel. By the time they'd finished at 0530hrs the following morning (June 8), one Ranger had died on the operating table of wounds, and one German prisoner-of-war had been treated for minor injuries.

Destroyers *Satterlee* (DD-626), *Baldwin* (DD-624), and *Nelson* (DD-623) viewed from heavy cruiser *Quincy* (CA-71) at Belfast, Northern Ireland, on May 14, 1944. Although assigned slightly different missions, all these warships would participate in the bombardment of Omaha during the morning of D-Day. (NHHC 80-G-367828)

raising hell with the men on the beach, and we can't have any more of that! We must stop it!" As the 1994 article *Destroyers at Normandy* aptly describes: "This was the hour of crisis."

By 1036hrs, *Frankford* had maneuvered deep inshore at Beach Easy Red, in the vicinity of Exit E-1. With its optical rangefinder at maximum elevation, *Frankford* registered a US tank near the surf line firing at a concealed target on the bluff, range 400yds. *Frankford*'s gunnery officer recalled: "We immediately followed up with a 5-inch salvo. The tank gunner flipped open his hatch, looked around at us, waved, dropped back in the tank, and fired at another target."

Frankford was accompanied 800yds off Easy Red by the destroyer *Doyle*. At 1100hrs, *Doyle* observed:

Enemy machine gun emplacement on side of steep hill at west end of beach Fox Red, enfilading landing beach. Fired two half [two-gun] salvos. Target destroyed. Shifted fire to casemate at top of hill, fired two half salvos, target destroyed. Army troops begin slow advance uphill from beach. Maneuvering ship to stay in position against current which is running west at 2.8 knots. Flood tide.[19]

An official US Army history reported: "All along the beach, infantry pinned at the sea wall and engineers trying to get at the draws to carry out their mission were heartened by this intervention."[20]

About 5,000 men had landed at Omaha Beach by 0900hrs. After initially remaining largely ignorant of the disaster unfolding at the water's edge, US Army generals had begun to slowly grasp the heavy casualties and destruction that had become increasingly apparent. The chaotic and traumatic circumstances at Omaha meant that extremely few messages were being received reporting the situation, as three-quarters of the 116th RCT's radios had been lost or destroyed. What little information senior officers offshore received was often well behind the actual events at the beach, making it nearly impossible for these Army generals, over the horizon in the transport anchorage, to grasp that the tide of battle might already be turning at Omaha.

In growing desperation US V Corps commander Major-General Gerow dispatched a DUKW with his assistant chief-of-staff, Colonel Benjamin Talley, to personally investigate the beach. Talley closed to within 500yds of Omaha

19 All excerpts from *Destroyers at Normandy* Naval, Historical Foundation (1994)
20 *CMH Pub 100-111 Omaha Beachhead*

and reported that US troops were pinned down by heavy German fire from the bluffs, and that the beach was so jammed with traffic that follow-on craft were unable to get ashore and were instead "milling around like cattle."

"I gained the impression," Bradley later recalled, "that our forces had suffered an irreversible catastrophe, that there was little hope that we could force the beach."[21] By 1100hrs, Bradley began seriously considering pulling out of Omaha and landing his remaining troops at other sectors. Kirk thus informed Moon that some of Omaha's remaining forces afloat might get transferred over to Utah. Moon admitted to his senior beach officer, Captain James Arnold, that "the show on Omaha didn't go quite according to plan …. [you may have to] take on a little extra burden." Moon then ordered his own Utah LSTs to close to within 4 miles of the beach, to make additional space for potential Omaha refugees.

Aboard Force O flagship USS *Ancon*, Captain Lorenzo Sabin (USN) thought that "everyone except Admiral Hall seemed to be tense, worried, and disturbed." Major-General Huebner, commander of the US 1st Division assaulting Omaha, expressed his anxiety to Hall. Hall simply responded: "I'm in command, and I'm not worried." Indeed, Hall remained quietly confident, knowing he had far more ground-based firepower still waiting to land than the German defenses had facing them. The only solution, Hall believed, was to simply keep landing more and more men and equipment, and the crisis would sort itself out. As Hall later observed: "The enemy was not [going to be able to] stop the landings."

However, Ramsay himself was disturbed enough about Omaha that around midmorning he quit his station off Sword and took a British destroyer to US flagship *Augusta* in the American zone. Summoning Kirk aboard, Ramsay demanded an explanation. "Don't worry, we'll get it sorted out," Kirk replied, with more confidence than he later admitted. Ramsay was not entirely convinced, but together they each downed a shot of whiskey and returned to their respective stations.

But the tide was beginning to turn. By 1100hrs, attack transport *Samuel Chase* (APA-26) reported it had successfully disembarked all its US 1st Division troops in 15 assault waves. A half hour later, Hall received another glimmer of good news: pockets of German troops were beginning to surrender. Moments later, a V Corps staff officer in a DUKW offshore reported US troops advancing up the Easy beach exit. The village of Colleville was taken at 1300hrs. Within half an hour, a general advance had begun up the Easy Red and Fox Green beaches, and by 1340hrs, Easy and Dog sectors, although still under fire, had been cleared of all live opposition.

According to Bradley:

The whole of D-day was for me a time of grave personal anxiety and frustration. …
Then at 1:30 P.M. I received a heartening message from [Major-General Leonard T.]

21 *Neptune*, Craig Symonds (2016)

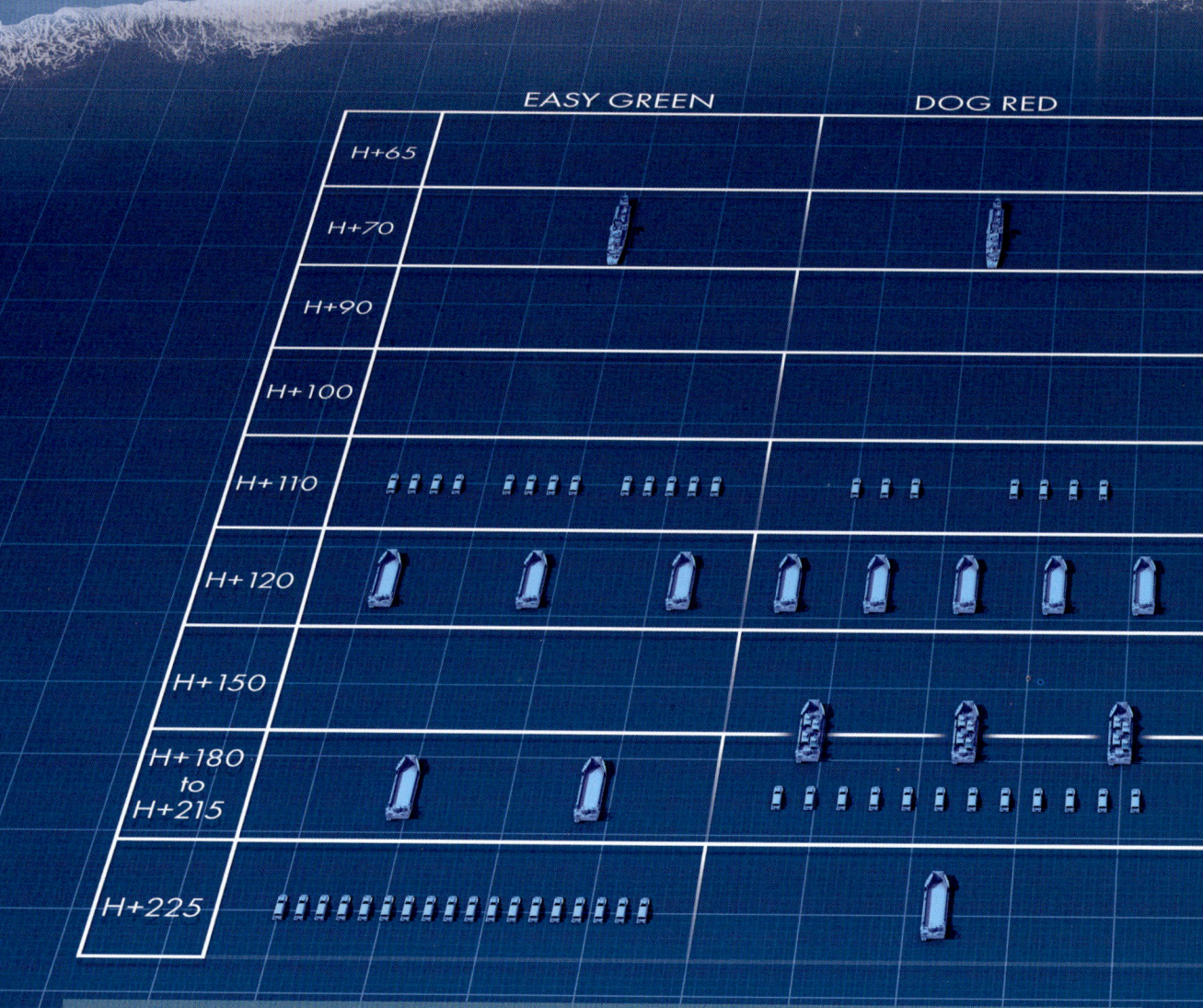

THE US 116TH RCT LANDINGS AT OMAHA FOLLOWING THE FIRST HOUR OF D-DAY

The rate of waves landing at Omaha was scheduled to gradually slow to allow the assault beach to be secured and also to avoid overly cluttering the landing zone.

Five minutes after the previous wave, at H+65, came seven LCA landing elements of the 5th Ranger Battalion at Beach Dog Green on the 116th RCT's right flank. After another five minutes came the first three LCIs carrying the 149th Engineer Beach Battalion, the 112th Engineer Battalion, and additional elements of the 116th RCT's headquarters, the first elements having been landed at H+60. Landing alongside the LCIs, on Beach Dog Green were eight LCAs carrying elements of the 5th Ranger Battalion, and two LCTs and one LCM carrying additional elements of the 121st Engineer Battalion.

Twenty minutes later came five LCTs of the 8th Armored's 58th Field Artillery Battalion. Aboard the LCTs were M7 Priest 105mm howitzers. These would land at Beach Dog White and were the only landing craft of the H+90 wave. The next wave, ten minutes later at H+100, was a single LCI carrying the 6th Special Engineering Brigade; this LCI would also be landing at Beach Dog White.

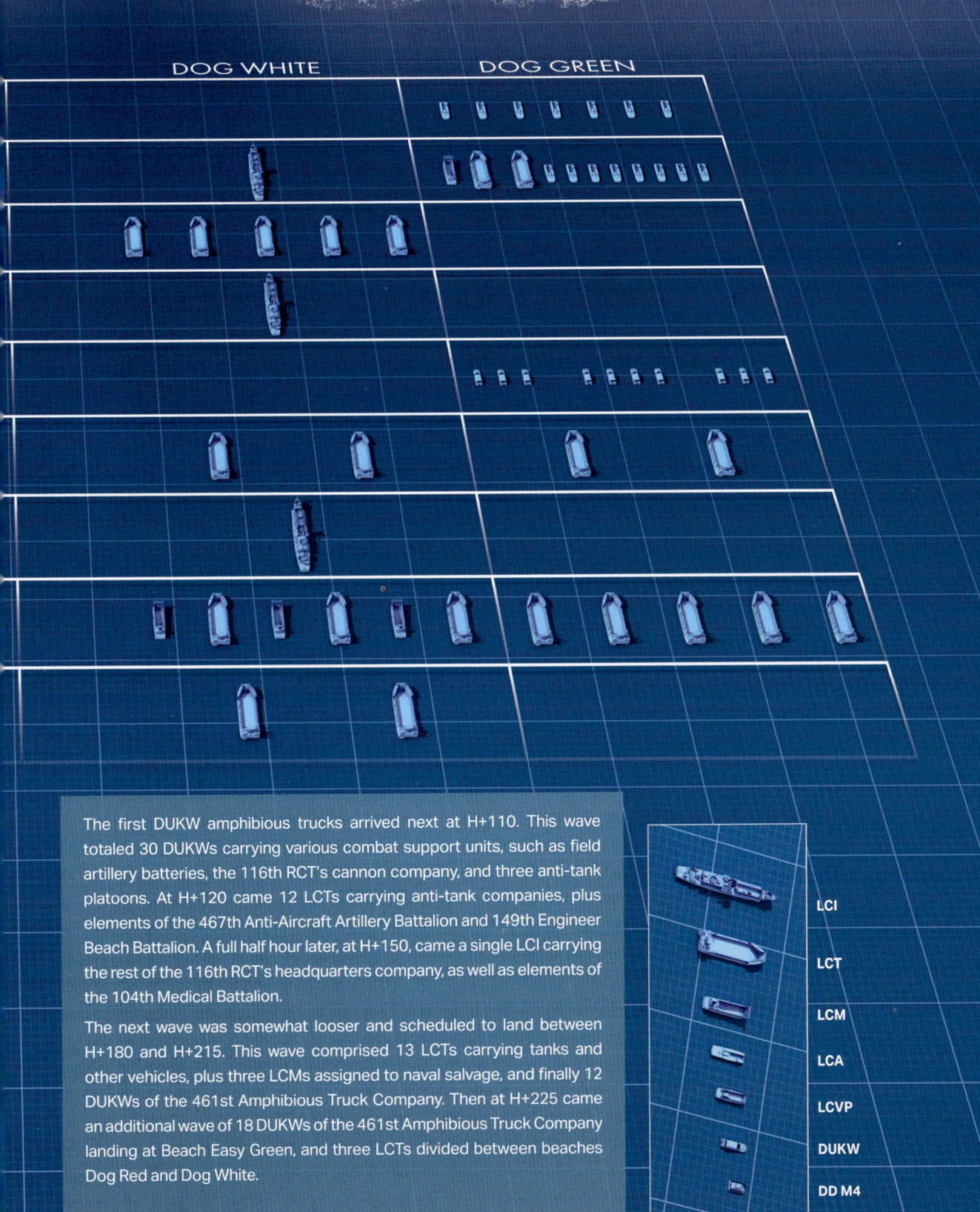

DOG WHITE DOG GREEN

The first DUKW amphibious trucks arrived next at H+110. This wave totaled 30 DUKWs carrying various combat support units, such as field artillery batteries, the 116th RCT's cannon company, and three anti-tank platoons. At H+120 came 12 LCTs carrying anti-tank companies, plus elements of the 467th Anti-Aircraft Artillery Battalion and 149th Engineer Beach Battalion. A full half hour later, at H+150, came a single LCI carrying the rest of the 116th RCT's headquarters company, as well as elements of the 104th Medical Battalion.

The next wave was somewhat looser and scheduled to land between H+180 and H+215. This wave comprised 13 LCTs carrying tanks and other vehicles, plus three LCMs assigned to naval salvage, and finally 12 DUKWs of the 461st Amphibious Truck Company. Then at H+225 came an additional wave of 18 DUKWs of the 461st Amphibious Truck Company landing at Beach Easy Green, and three LCTs divided between beaches Dog Red and Dog White.

LCI

LCT

LCM

LCA

LCVP

DUKW

DD M4

Gerow: "Troops formerly pinned down on beaches ... advancing up heights behind beaches." ... The situation everywhere on the beach was still grave, but our troops had forced one or two of the draws and were inciting inland. Based on their report, I gave up any thought of abandoning Omaha Beach.[22]

Nevertheless, Bradley later told Montgomery: "Someday I'll tell General Eisenhower just how close it was those first few hours."

By early afternoon, reinforcements were beginning to arrive. At 1530hrs, Follow-up Force B's Convoy B-2, comprising LCI(L)s and Landing Ship, Dock HMS *Oceanway*, stood to in the Transport Area and was directed to anchorages near the beach. Assault Groups O-1, O-2, and O-3 were ordered to provide landing craft to help unload. At 1540hrs, *Oceanway* began closing on Omaha to discharge its 20 LCMs loaded with M4 Sherman tanks. Twenty minutes later, Convoys O-3 and B-1 both arrived off Omaha. However, according to the commander of LCI(L)-542, even at 1830hrs,

"The [Omaha] beachhead did not appear well organized. There was only one visible beach marking; no shore parties were in evidence where this ship landed. There was little traffic control off the beach, and no channels were noticeable. LCI(L)s, LCTs, and other craft maneuvered haphazardly, frequently cutting across lines of approach."[23]

By 1700hrs, Kirk had established naval defensive sectors for the American beachheads. Drawing largely from D-Day fire support ships, Kirk formed an Area Screen that initially comprised nine destroyers, three destroyer-escorts, nine Patrol Craft, six British gunboats, and several PT boat groups, all under Captain Harry Sanders in the destroyer *Franklin*. These vessels were stationed 600yds apart on the "Mason" and "Dixie" lines established on either end of Omaha Beach. The Area Screen would patrol the assault area in force for the next 28 days, greatly dissuading strong or effective resistance from German air or naval counterattacks.

By late afternoon on D-Day, the US Army had begun to land some of its own field artillery, and most of five regiments of the 1st and 29th Divisions were ashore at Utah and Omaha. By 1900hrs, Major-General Huebner had established his 1st Division headquarters on Omaha. Huebner was followed shortly afterwards by Major-General Gerow, who established his own US V Corps command post ashore.

A damaged and smoking LCVP-16 from USS *Samuel Chase* (APA-26) limps its way into Omaha Beach on the morning of June 6, 1944. The smoke is from a burning hand grenade set off by a German machine-gun bullet. (NARA 26-G-2342)

22 *Neptune,* Craig Symonds (2016)
23 *Neptune,* Craig Symonds (2016)

Nevertheless, well-disguised German artillery positions continued to land "sporadic but heavy shelling" on the Omaha beachhead throughout the afternoon and evening of D-Day. An Omaha destroyer officer observed that German fire was "evidently controlled by observers watching the beaches" from houses on cliffs and inland hills that had never been targeted by US planners. However, by the time we realized this our troops were advancing and we were unable to obtain permission to shell any but a few of the most obvious. It was most galling and depressing to lie idly a few hundred yards off the beaches and watch our troops, tanks, landing boats, and motor vehicles being heavily shelled and not be able to fire a shot to help them just because we had no information as to what to shoot at and were unable to detect the source of the enemy fire.[26]

26 *Amphibious Operations. Invasion of Northern France. Western Naval Task Force.* (US Fleet)

Point-blank gunfire support on Omaha Beach   (overleaf)

By 0900hrs on June 6, the Omaha Beach situation had degenerated into a burning, smoking disaster, with troops stalled ashore, and wrecked and beached landing craft piling up on the beach and just offshore. In the midmorning low gray overcast, the seas were high and choppy. The scene was generally one of utter chaos.

In a desperate attempt to retrieve the catastrophe unfolding on shore, the DesDiv-18 flagship, Gleaves-class destroyer USS *Frankford* (DD-497) is shown charging into the maelstrom and risking grounding itself on the shallow bottom. *Frankford* closed to less than 1,000yds of the shoreline to deliver withering pointblank fire from its 5in. guns and antiaircraft guns, directly at German pillboxes and emplacements that were largely camouflaged and concealed if they were even visible at all.

The sea off Omaha Beach and around *Frankford* is churned up by German machine-gun fire and geysers from German guns shooting at both *Frankford* and the American troops and landing craft in general. *Frankford* is risking not just pointblank fire from German coastal artillery and machine guns, but submerged naval mines and beach obstacles along with the heavy detritus of torn-up and traffic-jammed landing craft and vehicles.

Frankford's skipper, Lieutenant-Commander Semmes, decided that "we should go in for a closer look. The tide was in our favor at the moment. Navigating by fathometer and seaman's eye, he took us in close enough to put our optical rangefinder, ranging on the bluff above the beach, against the stops – 300–400yds away." [24]

By 1036hrs, *Frankford* was maneuvering deep inshore at Omaha's Beach Easy Red. *Frankford*'s gunnery officer observed a US tank near the surf line firing up the high bluff at a hidden target 400yds away. He later commented:

We immediately followed up with a 5in. salvo. The tank gunner flipped open his hatch, looked around at us, waved, dropped back in the tank, and fired at another target. For the next few minutes he was our fire-control party. Our rangefinder optics could examine the spots where his shells hit. By this time, we knew that none of our troops were on the hill, so we used the rangefinder to pick out targets, including apparently at least one artillery emplacement. We did have the satisfaction of seeing our soldiers take some prisoners out of one of those bunkers.

Once *Frankford* had expended its bombardment ammunition, the destroyer returned to its screening station – "but not before seeing our troops moving up the hill towards the crest."[25]

24 *Destroyers at Normandy* Naval, Historical Foundation(1994)
25 *Destroyers at Normandy* Naval, Historical Foundation(1994)

Nevertheless, there is strong evidence to suggest that the unexpectedly aggressive actions of US destroyers had saved the Omaha landings. Sergeant Barton Davis, writing later to *Frankford* skipper Captain Semmes, recalled:

How well I remember your ship coming in so close. I thought then as I do now that it was one brave thing to come in so close. … Your ship not only knocked out the pillbox but also the mortar positions above us. … I always thought how great it would be to tell the Captain of that ship how grateful I am.

A second combat engineer wrote to *Frankford*'s crew:

There is no question, at least in my mind, if you had not come in as close as you did, exposing yourself to God only knows how much, that I would not have survived the night. I truly believe that in the absence of the damage you inflicted on the German emplacements, the only way any GI was going to leave Omaha was in a mattress cover or as a prisoner of war.

After inspecting Omaha's battered defenses, the US 1st Division's chief-of-staff, Colonel S. B. Mason, wrote to Rear Admiral Hall:

I am now firmly convinced that our supporting naval fire got us in; that without that gunfire we positively could not have crossed the beaches … I looked over the destruction of German pillboxes, fortified houses, and gun positions, and in all cases it was apparent that naval guns had worked on them … if ever we have to do another of these jobs, we will all hope of being teamed with the XI Amphib, for planning and execution. General Huebner concurs in the above.

Bradley agreed:

Here I must give unstinting praise to the U.S. Navy. … The Navy saved our hides. Twelve destroyers moved in close to the beach, heedless of shallow water, mines, enemy fire and other obstacles, to give us close support. The main batteries of these gallant ships became our sole artillery. … When [General Gerow] got ashore that night to establish his V Corps command posts, his first message to me was emotional: "Thank God for the U.S. Navy."

The Western Naval Task Force's major D-Day ship losses had been minesweeper *Osprey* (AM-56), lost late on June 5 to a naval mine; destroyer *Corry* (DD-463) to coast artillery and a naval mine; 12 LCTs, one LCF, and five LCI(L)s to naval mines; one LCT to foundering; one LCT and two LCI(L)s to shore batteries; and PC-1261 to shellfire or naval mines.

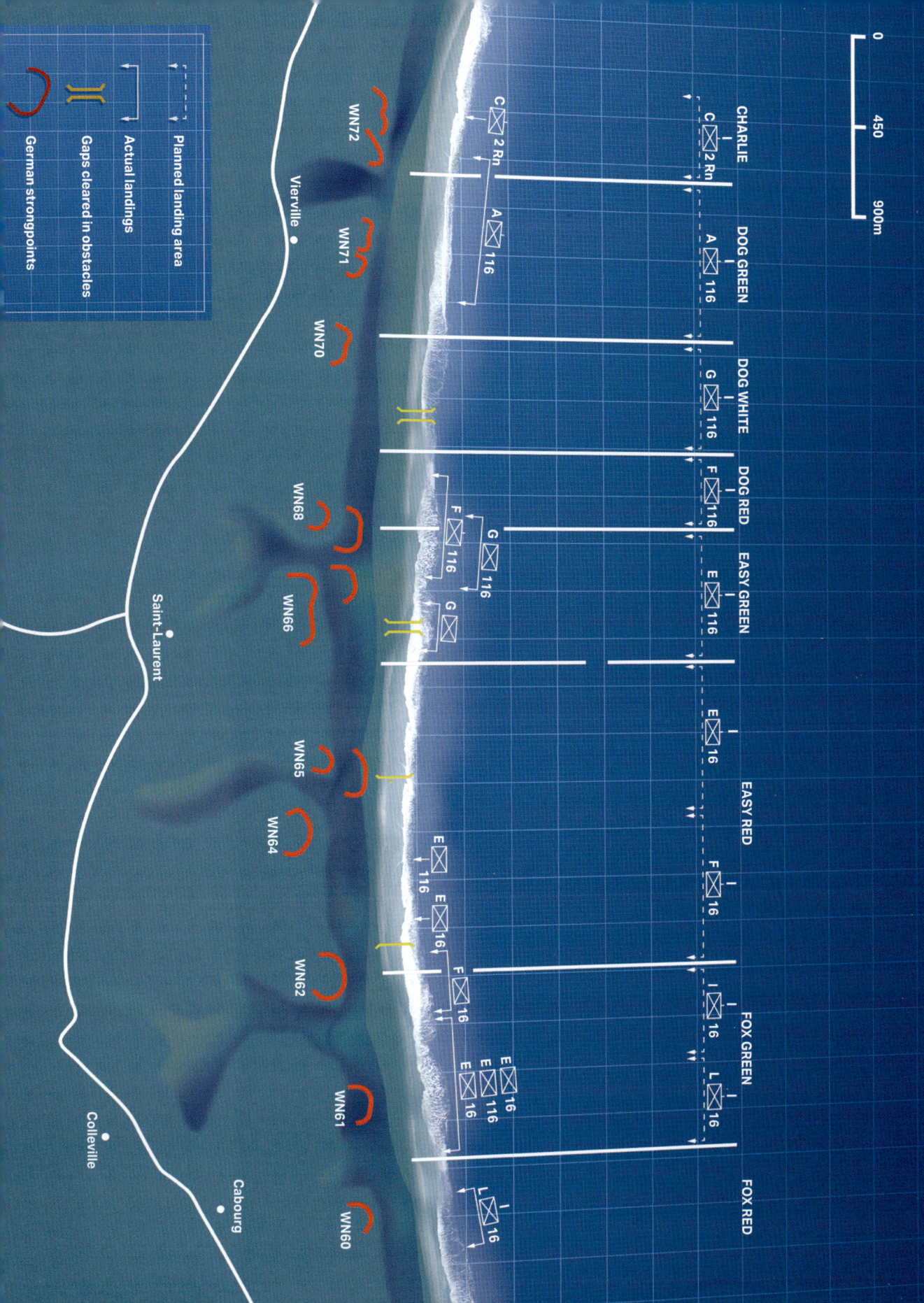

Rear Admiral Carleton F. Bryant, commander of Bombardment Group C at Omaha. Bryant's perhaps belated order for all gunships to close on the beaches and rain maximum havoc was one of the decisive moments of the Omaha landings, although many destroyers had already taken the initiative on gunfire support some time earlier. (NH 51564)

The northern summer sun finally set at 2207hrs. It was followed by a bright full moon that garishly illuminated the beaches. Years later, Bradley would write:

By nightfall, the situation had swung in our favor. Personal heroism and the U.S. Navy had carried the day. We had by then landed close to 35,000 men and held a sliver of corpse-littered beach five miles long and about one and a half miles deep. To wrest that sliver from the enemy had cost us possibly 2,500 casualties. There was now no thought of giving it back.[27]

Follow-on operations, June 7–15, 1944

As night fell, however dramatic and ultimately triumphant D-Day had been, US officers knew that *Neptune*'s ultimate success or failure remained undecided. Indeed, as COSSAC had predicted in 1943, "The surprise assault would no doubt win the first round."

Aside from a midmorning strafing run by two Fw-190s, German air activity on D-Day was nil. But the Luftwaffe immediately flew in 1,000 aircraft from Germany and Italy to mount counterattacks. These were mostly fighters intended to strafe the beaches, but 45 were torpedo-carrying Ju-88 bombers. The Luftwaffe finally began launching attacks on the invasion fleet during the night of June 6–7, beginning just before midnight. An estimated 22 Luftwaffe aircraft attacked shipping off Omaha. No hits were scored, although a bomb from a Ju-88 just missed the battleship *Arkansas*. Two German aircraft were reported shot down, one by air cover and another by destroyer-escort USS *Maloy* (DE-791). Indeed, between June 6 and 17, German air strikes would mostly come at night.

Allied battleships, cruisers, and destroyers would demonstrate excellent anti-aircraft fire discipline throughout *Neptune*. However, within several days of the landings, merchant ships in the Assault Area would be prohibited from firing at all during the hours of darkness, while small naval ships were prohibited from firing in the dark unless directly attacked. By D+7, fire discipline within the Assault Area would markedly improve.

Minesweeping operations would continue throughout the post-assault period, as Allied minesweepers continued to widen safe channels and beach zones as much as possible. By July 3, minesweepers had swept 261 naval mines in the American sector alone. However, naval mines would remain the primary scourge of Allied shipping off Normandy.

Early on D-Day, Utah commander Rear Admiral Moon had announced: "The initial action has been won. The next phase will be a race between the build-up of the Allied forces and the movement of the enemy reserves." Indeed, the third and final Force B follow-on convoy of four transports arrived off

27 All extracts from *Amphibious Operations. Invasion of Northern France. Western Naval Task Force* (US Fleet)

Omaha Beach at 0600hrs on June 7. While approaching Omaha at 0820hrs, troop transport *Susan B. Anthony* (AP-272) struck a delayed-action magnetic or sonic mine. It immediately began sinking and was evacuated, with LCI-496 taking on 434 men in just 15 minutes. Fleet tug USS *Pinto* (AT-90) and two destroyers also assisted, and by the time *Susan B. Anthony* sank 10 miles off the coast at 1010hrs, all 2,689 personnel aboard had been rescued, still a world record for the most people rescued from a sinking ship without loss of life. A mere 45 had been wounded. Similarly, US freighter *Francis Harrington* was en route to Normandy in convoy EMB-2 when it too struck a naval mine. Six were killed, but the *Francis Harrington* still managed to discharge its cargo and passengers at Omaha.

Barely an hour after the *Susan B. Anthony* had been hit, minesweeper USS *Tide* (AM-125) struck a naval mine off Utah that mortally wounded its skipper. Fellow minesweepers USS *Pheasant* and USS *Threat* began rescuing *Tide*'s survivors, but when USS *Swift* took *Tide* under tow, *Tide* broke in half and sank. That same day, June 7, would see LCT-436, LCT-458, LCT-586, and LCI-232 all sunk by German mines. The destroyers *Jeffers* (DD-621) and *Harding* (DD-625) both suffered their own damage; *Jeffers* slight damage to German shellfire and *Harding* more extensive damage when it ran aground. Off Utah, LCT(A)-2310 was also hit and damaged by German coastal fire.

Nevertheless, by 1200hrs on June 7, the American follow-up convoys B-3 and U-4 had arrived in the Western sector, along with the first of 28 sunken causeways and four large barges for the American Mulberry at Omaha. In the subsequent hours, five US follow-on convoys would arrive, including two loaded with ammunition. By evening on June 7, almost all of Force O and Force B had been successfully landed at Omaha.

The following day, June 8, saw Bombardon units being connected, Mulberry headquarters ships arrive, 14 blockships sunk for Mulberry A, and four 1,000-ton ammunition barges arrive in the WNTF area. However, by midnight on June 8, only 6,614 tons of supplies had been landed, or less than 27 percent of that scheduled. Within 48 hours, this would rise to 21,800 tons, or 48 percent of that anticipated. By D+4 (June 10), it was expected that the cross-Channel buildup rhythm would settle at 58,000 men and 8,000 vehicles being landed daily across the full Anglo-American beachhead.

LST-388 and battleship *Texas* are seen on June 7, 1944. LST-388 carried 361 personnel and 70 vehicles of the 187th Field Artillery battalion to Normandy, as well as towing a Rhino ferry, before arriving and anchoring off Omaha at 1215hrs, June 7. (US Navy)

Supply landing sectors at Omaha were marked by large signs, appropriately color- and number-coded and mounted high on the bluffs so they were visible at sea. Utah's extraordinarily flat terrain required its sectors to be marked by floating barrage balloons. Transports and Liberty ships remained at sea while their passengers and cargo were ferried ashore. Personnel were carried by LCVPs and LCTs, while Rhino ferries shuttled vehicles and heavy freight. Only two LSTs had attempted to land on Omaha on June 6 and both had been badly damaged by German artillery. One, LST-133, had successfully beached and discharged tanks and other cargo while embarking wounded. But LST-133 had been unable to extricate itself off the beach and was stranded. LSTs loaded with vehicles could land and retract quickly because the vehicles could simply drive out. However, LSTs carrying freight took much longer to unload and often had to sit through an entire tide cycle until a new high tide could free them from the shore. Because Omaha was still in easy range of German artillery on June 7, Ramsay forbade the unloading of LSTs directly on the beach at Omaha "except in an emergency," despite allowing it in the other four sectors.

Supplies were sometimes dumped at low tide, meaning they would be inundated if not retrieved before the next high tide. This could be avoided with DUKWs, which could ferry ordnance from miles offshore directly to supply dumps inland. In fact, DUKWs had been expected to land the first hour of D-Day, but the only DUKW that attempted to do so had been knocked out. Some had made it ashore in the early afternoon, but most DUKWs earmarked for D-Day had been held offshore to land on June 7. With both trucks and ferry craft in such short supply, the versatile DUKWs were badly overworked. Many were burdened with twice their designed load weight. Some DUKWs were launched up to 15nm offshore, but these often ran out of fuel, starving their bilge pumps and sinking them.

Neptune plans had envisioned Omaha as the predominant beach for receiving supplies in the American sector. However, the near-disaster on D-Day meant the beach was already far behind schedule. Omaha was to have received 2,400 tons of supplies on D-Day, but instead received only 100 tons. Vehicle wreckage would choke Omaha until June 9, by which time only 4,581 tons of supplies had been received.

The night of June 7–8 saw roughly 100 Luftwaffe sorties against the invasion fleet. Around midnight, some 50 German aircraft were detected overhead, laying mines and dropping bombs. Negligible damage was inflicted, although an Allied night fighter shot down a Ju-88. Throughout the first week of *Neptune*, the Luftwaffe would fly 1,683 strike sorties against the full *Neptune* invasion fleet. The Luftwaffe's main weapon was naval mines, but "sporadic and harassing" bombing and strafing attacks against shipping and beaches would also take place, including attacks by Henschel Hs-293 radio-controlled bombs. A German bomber could carry two each of these and launch them from several miles away. Upon registering the bombs' telltale radio tone, Allied ships would transmit "Vermin!" and begin flooding the radio with jamming signals. However, around 0100hrs on June 8, a glide-bomb from an He-177 struck destroyer USS *Meredith* (DD-726) near the waterline. *Meredith* lost power, went dead in the water, and was ordered abandoned at 0250hrs. Attempts to salvage it were unsuccessful, and it suddenly broke in half and sank at 1010hrs on June 9.

A coaster drying out at Utah Beach, helping to supply US VII Corps immediately inland. Although lacking in glamor, coastal shipping borrowed from British shores proved invaluable at filling out the Western Naval Task Force's lift capacity. (US Navy)

Indeed, June 8 would prove quite eventful. At 0130hrs, five German S-boats from Cherbourg claimed to have scored three torpedo hits in an attack against a destroyer and cruiser off Utah, but the WNTF recorded nothing. An hour later, these same S-boats were damaged by two British frigates and British MTBs out of Portsmouth, but successfully returned to port.

A few hours later, LST-499 weighed anchor off Utah and proceeded closer inshore to expedite its unloading. Suddenly, a German influence mine detonated beneath its port quarter, knocking out both engines and sending seawater rushing through blasted hull plating. With its pumps disabled, LST-499 settled by the stern and within ten minutes was abandoned.

At 0830hrs the same morning, the destroyer USS *Glennon* (DD-620) hit a naval mine while deploying to its gunfire support station. Within 30 minutes, it was under tow by two minesweepers while under German artillery fire. Steaming to assist *Glennon*, at 0840hrs destroyer-escort USS *Rich* (DE-695) struck the first of three naval mines in quick succession. *Rich* sank within 15 minutes of hitting the first mine, losing 79 killed and missing. Meanwhile, *Glennon* had gone hard aground. Salvage operations proceeded the next day, but by June 10 *Glennon* would be hit by three consecutive German artillery barrages, forcing its men to abandon ship for good. *Glennon* sank late that evening, having suffered 25 dead and 38 wounded. Nor were smaller auxiliaries immune on June 8.

While escorting Mulberry units to Omaha, auxiliary netlayer HMS *Minster* struck a naval mine and quickly sank, losing 58 dead – most of its complement.

Finally, at 2330hrs on June 8, ten S-boats departed Cherbourg to raid Allied reinforcement convoys and lay mines near the Saint-Marcouf islands. They were discovered on radar by Captain Sanders' screen. At 0036hrs on June 9, the destroyers *Baldwin* and *Hambleton* opened fire from 7,500yds, forcing the S-boats to promptly flee at 30 knots. However, that same night, other S-boats struck a five-ship convoy in mid-Channel under Portsmouth command, sinking LST-376 and LST-314, with LST-314 taking half its complement with it.

The USN had always wanted to unload ships as fast as possible, but US Army troops in desperate firefights inland understandably made frantic requests for specific items, namely ammunition. Hall made his case in an appeal to Bradley, and on June 10 Bradley authorized the USN to "unload all ships as fast as possible regardless of priorities." That same day, Ramsay authorized LSTs to begin landing directly on Omaha Beach, declaring: "Empty the ships and priorities will take care of themselves."

On June 10 off Utah, a bomb struck Liberty ship SS *Charles Morgan*. Its stern settled on the seafloor, but the ship was later salvaged. Early on June 11, five fleet tugs were towing a heavy Mulberry unit across the Channel to Omaha when they were attacked by S-boats at 0215hrs. One torpedoed fleet tug USS *Partridge*, which sank in less than a minute with 32 dead. Moments later, the S-boats attacked a nearby LST convoy, damaging but not sinking LST-538. Later that day, LST-496 was sunk by a naval mine, while LCI(L)-219 was bombed and sunk en route to the Utah area. Meanwhile, overnight on June 11–12, attacking S-boats blew the stern off destroyer USS *Nelson* (DD-623), which was subsequently towed to Portsmouth.

Meanwhile, late on June 11, the destroyer USS *Thompson* (DD-627) had suddenly been ordered back to Portsmouth. The following morning, the *Thompson* was boarded by an American VIP party that included Admiral

Buckley-class destroyer-escort USS *Rich* (DE-695), struck by a naval mine off Normandy and sinking on June 8, 1944. This was the second mine it had struck; the first mine blew its stern off. The Western Naval Task Force's destroyer-escorts provided anti-submarine escort as well as gunfire support duties. (NH 44312)

Ernest J. King, General George C. Marshall, General Dwight D. Eisenhower, and General Henry "Hap" Arnold. *Thompson* then ferried the officers across the Channel to Omaha, where they had lunch ashore with Bradley and Gerow, then promptly ferried them back to Portsmouth.

The next day, June 13, LCT-967 and minesweeper MMS-229 were sunk by naval mines. However, the following day, the Germans began demolishing Cherbourg's port facilities. German naval forces were forced to withdraw, and while the German minefields obviously remained, Kriegsmarine surface attacks on the WNTF largely ended. Nevertheless, that night (June 14–15), Luftwaffe bombers dropped two rows of floating flares into the assault area, a new aerial tactic. But over the following nights, prepared US PT Boats quickly machine-gunned and sank them before any bombs could be accurately dropped.

German artillery fire had continued to hamper American unloading at both beaches, but the last German battery capable of reaching Utah had been overrun on June 12. By then (D+6), the American reinforcement of the beaches had entered a new phase. The initial beach dump phase ended, as inland dumps were now operational. In its place began the new beach maintenance dump phase. Transfer points were now established on the beaches, with crane facilities to transfer netted cargo from DUKWs to trucks and thus make inland DUKW expeditions unnecessary. The sole exception was ammunition dumps; because of shortages, these were consolidated into a single dump near Formigny. It was also now that the Americans began unloading supplies all night under floodlights. Further milestones were reached in the following days, with the US Army landing its tenth division at Normandy on June 14, the same day First US Army took control of all inland dumps. Meanwhile, the nine-day backlog of ships was finally cleared on June 15, when Hall could claim: "All previous records for stores landed on the Force O beaches was broken on each successive day."

However, naval losses had been significant. The combined total of WNTF warships sunk or destroyed by June 17, 1944, came to one transport, three destroyers, one destroyer-escort, two minesweepers, one patrol craft, one motor minesweeper, one trawler, one tug, one danlayer, one seaplane tender, four LSTs, nine LCI(L)s, one LCF, and 25 LCTs. Small landing craft lost or destroyed were eight LCMs, one LCS(S), 81 LCVPs, 17 LCAs, and seven LCP(L) Smokes. A fifth LST would be sunk two days later when LST-523 hit a naval mine off Pointe du Hoc.

Alexander P. Russo's 1944 gouache-on-paper painting, In the Transport Area, depicts a nocturnal Luftwaffe attack over the Allied Normandy bridgehead. The lazily dropping yellow light sources are Luftwaffe flares designed to light the entire seascape below for targeting Allied shipping. Contrasting with them are the sharp orange-red blasts of Allied antiaircraft tracers fired back through Normandy's typically thick and low overcast. (NHHC 88-198-P)

The June 19–22 Channel storm

By now, Omaha was coming into its own. The official US Army history states:

In contrast to the confusion and chaos of D Day, activities at Omaha Beach by the end of the second week resembled the operations of a major port. Except for three or four wrecked craft, beaches were clear, and minefields behind the sea wall were slowly being cleared. Additional roads were pushed through the shingle pile, and exits were blasted through the sea wall.

Seemingly just as importantly, the Omaha Mulberry port became fully operational on June 16; a single LST could now completely unload in one hour, compared to 12 hours before.

By the evening of June 18, the Americans had unloaded 314,514 troops, 41,000 vehicles, and 116,000 tons of supplies over Utah and Omaha beaches. But within hours, Normandy would get slammed by the worst midsummer Channel storm in 40 years. Around midnight on June 18–19, a strong northeast wind with heavy rain began to hammer the assault beaches. By morning, the wind had increased to 22 knots, with gusts reaching 33 knots. Powered by a 90–125nm fetch of Channel, the sea state built suddenly into a Force 6–8 storm that accentuated Normandy's already severe tides and suspended all Mulberry unloading on the afternoon of June 19.

LCTs, landing craft, and other small vessels were driven ashore and wrecked. On June 20, a drifting salvage barge and five LCTs rammed Mulberry A's already-disintegrating center pontoon causeway. Just-arriving Phoenix caissons floated out of control from their tugs and either beached or were scuttled. By late June 20, three of four Lobnitz piers were taking on water, while 25 of the huge steel "bombardons" of the outer breakwater broke free, destroying themselves and anything in their way as they inevitably rammed their way to shore, a scene one British officer described as "unutterable chaos." However, most of the Gooseberry breakwaters survived the maelstrom and sheltered several hundred landing craft throughout the tempest.

By the storm's end on June 22, "the Omaha beaches were a shambles of stranded and wrecked craft, coasting vessels, barges, and Mulberry fragments. General Bradley 'was appalled by the desolation.'"[28] Naval losses off Mulberry A came to five LSTs, one LSI(H), 13 LCI(L)s, and about 50 LCTs. Mulberry A was so thoroughly wrecked that Ramsay and Kirk wrote it off, transferring most surviving parts to the British Mulberry B, which had survived the storm in better shape.

28 *The Invasion of France and Germany* Naval Institute Press (2011)

USS LST-325 and USS LST-388 are stranded at low tide while supplying forces ashore on June 12, 1944. Among the details visible on LST-325 are kedge anchors, propellers, rudders, and two single 40mm Bofors antiaircraft weapons in gun tubs. (US Navy)

Post-storm logistics over the beaches

Many ferry craft had been wrecked by the storm. However, even on the storm's worst day, June 22, Utah and Omaha received a combined 1,359 tons of supplies. The amphibious DUKWs proved invaluable, as they had been safely parked ashore and were ready to operate immediately. In fact, more DUKWs were operational after the storm than before it, the three-day downtime having allowed additional maintenance.

To provide an emergency supply for the ground forces, the WNTF had loaded 16 1,000-ton capacity barges with ammunition and towed them across the Channel. These had been beached at high tide (including six on D-Day) and were unloaded by trucks in between tides. With their reserve stocks of ammunition, the beached barges proved critical during the storm.

The WNTF had landed three US infantry divisions over the beaches on D-Day. Two more were delivered on D+2, followed by the first US armored division on D+4. By June 22 (D+16), a total of 11 US divisions had been landed in Normandy, including two armored divisions. July would see the arrival of seven more US divisions.

American logistical power makes its presence felt at Omaha Beach in mid-June 1944. Many LSTs are beached and debarking, including USS LST-532, USS LST-262, USS LST-310, USS LST-533, and USS LST-524. The LSTs are accompanied by protective barrage balloons. A halftrack convoy is forming up to move inland, while many other ships to seawards await their own turn to discharge. (NHHC 26-G-2517)

US ARMY BUILDUP IN NORMANDY, JUNE 1944	
Arrival date	US Division
June 6	1st, 4th, 29th Infantry
June 8	2nd, 90th Infantry
June 10	2nd Armored
June 12	9th Infantry
June 14	79th Infantry
June 16	30th Infantry
June 21	83rd Infantry
June 22	3rd Armored

In hindsight, the sudden early destruction of Mulberry A proved a long-term blessing in disguise. By July 5 (D+30), the surviving Mulberry harbor in the British sector had maxed out at 6,750 tons of supplies per day. In contrast, the Americans were now unloading 9,200 tons per day straight over the beaches (1,200 tons at Omaha and 8,000 at Utah). By August 4 (D+60), this daily figure would soar to 16,000 tons (10,000 at Omaha and 6,000 at Utah). According to an official US Army history: "The planners obviously underrated the capacities of open beaches. The tremendous tonnage capacities subsequently developed at both Utah and Omaha were without doubt one of the most significant and gratifying features of the entire *Overlord* operation."[29]

Between June 7 and June 30, a total of 180 transports, 570 Liberty ships, 372 LCIs, 905 LSTs, 1,442 LCTs, and 788 coastal freighters had arrived at the *Neptune* assault area, equivalent to one-third of the United Kingdom's normal annual import capacity.

Cherbourg naval fire support, June 25, 1944

Kirk's WNTF had continued to give naval fire support since D-Day. On June 7, the battleship *Nevada* and cruisers *Tuscaloosa* and *Quincy* had notably assisted US troops driving inland from Utah by bombarding German bridges, guns, and troop concentrations. Force O provided naval gunfire supporting the fragile Omaha beachhead. Most importantly, on June 7, naval gunfire helped stave off a powerful German counterattack against Pointe du Hoc, which reclaimed much ground lost on D-Day and nearly drove the Rangers back into the sea.

Kirk's gunships continued to support Bradley's First US Army as it pushed into the difficult bocage country. However, as US troops moved deeper inland, there remained fewer appropriate targets for naval gunfire support, and on June 15 Kirk consolidated all bombardment ships under Deyo to handle the entire US sector. Three days later, Major-General Collins' US VII Corps cut off the heavily fortified Cotentin peninsula. Supporting the Cotentin's 40,000 German defenders were 20 casemated batteries, including three 280mm batteries and 12 batteries of 150mm or greater; these were accompanied by many 75mm and 88mm concentrations. Collins duly requested naval assistance in VII Corps' impending assault against Cherbourg.

The Cherbourg bombardment force, designated Task Force 129, sortied from Portland at 0430hrs on June 25. Group 1 was directly commanded by Deyo and comprised the battleship *Nevada*, cruisers *Tuscaloosa*, *Quincy*, *Glasgow*, and *Enterprise*, and six US destroyers. Group 2 was commanded by Bryant and consisted of the battleships *Texas* and *Arkansas*, plus five US destroyers.

Nevada's 14in. main guns are trained to port on the morning of June 25, 1944, as it prepares to bombard Cherbourg in support of the land-based advance into the city by the US VII Corps. *Nevada* was one of the earlier US battleships to be refloated at Pearl Harbor. *Nevada*'s first combat after resurrection was to provide fire support for the May 1943 liberation of Attu island off Alaska. (IWM A 24312)

29 *CMH Pub 7-2-1 Logistical Support of the Armies*

Clearing the route ahead of the bombardment force was the USN's Mine Squadron 7 and the Royal Navy's 9th Minesweeping Flotilla. Spitfires again provided air spotting, while P-38 Lightnings supplied fighter cover.

Cherbourg's most dangerous coastal battery was Battery Hamburg, located 6 miles east of the city and comprising four widely separated 280mm (11in.) guns in reinforced casemates surrounded by 88mm guns. The 280mm guns had a range of 40,000yds, while the battleships were ordered to engage from 28,000yds. As Group 1 steamed west to take on the Cherbourg port directly, Battery Hamburg was to be silenced by *Nevada*'s 14in. guns. *Texas* and *Arkansas* would then complete Battery Hamburg's destruction before joining Group 1 off Cherbourg.

However, worried about friendly fire, Collins suddenly tightened his directions. Deyo was now only to begin the bombardment at 1200hrs and was only to target three specific batteries, plus any targets called by shore fire control parties and any batteries that fired on his own ships. *Nevada*'s preliminary bombardment of Battery Hamburg was therefore canceled.

At noon, the bombardment force began steaming towards the Cherbourg approaches, stymied by the 5-knot speed of their leading minesweepers clearing open channels. The minesweepers were increasingly knocked off course by the strong local currents, frustrating their following gunships; *Nevada*, *Quincy*, *Tuscaloosa*, *Glasgow*, and *Enterprise* were all forced to reduce speed upon their approach. German guns at Querqueville, 3 miles west of Cherbourg, opened fire on the creeping flotilla at 1206hrs. Deyo's force increased speed and returned fire, with destroyers laying smoke. Within 20 minutes, every minesweeper in Deyo's force had been straddled by German salvos.

Collins' first fire support call came at 1212hrs. *Nevada* and *Quincy* hammered away for 25 minutes, then shifted fire to a second target near Querqueville before receiving yet another fire request from shore spotters. Meanwhile, Group 1's destroyers laid smoke and closed in on the Querqueville battery, which was now receiving fire from HMS *Glasgow* and HMS *Enterprise*. At 1251hrs, *Glasgow* was hit by a 150mm shell, but suffered no significant damage. Continued Allied fire temporarily silenced the Querqueville battery. Similarly, the destroyer *Ellyson* spotted fire coming from a battery near Gruchy. This was temporarily silenced by 54 rounds from *Glasgow*, but like most German guns that afternoon, the battery would repeatedly come back to life and have to be suppressed again.

Bryant's Group 2 – comprising *Texas*, *Arkansas*, and five destroyers – opened its assigned duel with Battery Hamburg. *Arkansas*, in contact with its fire support party, closed to 18,000yds, but could not connect with the target. *Texas* was still unable to raise its own fire support party and milled behind the minesweepers. Battery Hamburg now retaliated against Group 2, and German guns scored

German coast artillery shells fall a few hundred yards in front of USS *Quincy*'s bow off Cherbourg on June 25. The photo was taken from *Quincy*'s bridge. Commissioned on December 15, 1943, USS *Quincy* (CA-71) was a modern Baltimore-class heavy cruiser named after the New Orleans-class heavy cruiser that had been sunk off Savo Island on August 9, 1942. (NH 82515)

Cruisers HMS *Glasgow* (foreground) and USS *Quincy* (background) bombard heavy German artillery emplacements in the Cherbourg area on June 25, 1944. Both vessels saw brief wartime service in the Pacific, *Glasgow* at the beginning of the Pacific War and *Quincy* at the very end. (IWM A 24310)

against three US destroyers. The *Barton* and *Laffey* were struck by dud 240mm shells, but Battery Hamburg hit *O'Brien* in the bridge, killing 13, knocking out the radar, and forcing it to withdraw under the covering fire of its sister destroyers.

With the destroyers retreating, *Texas* began its famous one-on-one duel with Battery Hamburg just before 1300hrs. Making hard evasive maneuvers, *Texas* was repeatedly straddled by German salvos as numerous enemy shells just missed first its bow and then its stern. After 20 minutes, a second German battery opened up on *Texas*, catching the old dreadnought in a crossfire. Finally, a German 280mm shell hit *Texas'* upper conning tower and exploded, killing one and wounding 13. Still firing, *Texas* turned for open water.

Ten minutes before the scheduled end of the bombardment at 1330hrs, Deyo signaled: "Do you want more gunfire? Enemy batteries still active." During this time, the Querqueville battery had again opened fire and straddled *Emmons* four times before the destroyer retreated behind a smokescreen. At 1402hrs, a grateful Collins duly requested an hour-long extension to the bombardment, as by now VII Corps had nearly broken into Cherbourg.

The destroyer *Hambleton* began firing on an eight-gun battery of 88mms at the port's Fort des Flamand, but was forced to retreat under Battery Hamburg fire. *Quincy* then closed and took out the 88mm guns. Meanwhile, *Tuscaloosa* scored a direct hit on the Querqueville battery; by 1440hrs, Querqueville would finally be silenced after receiving several hundred shells from the task force.

At 1500hrs, Deyo's force began to withdraw, only to receive another fire call against casemated 75mm guns at Cherbourg's naval arsenal. As it retired, Deyo's flagship *Tuscaloosa* responded with accurate long-range 8in. salvos. By 1530hrs, the bombardment force had fully withdrawn. *Nevada* had been straddled 23 times, showering it with splinters, *Texas* had suffered a hit to the bridge, and the cruiser *Glasgow* and destroyers *O'Brien*, *Laffey*, and *Barton* had all reported damage from shell hits. Casualties to the bombardment force were 13 dead and 82 wounded. The most difficult German batteries had been those originally scheduled to be eliminated from long range.

US VII Corps captured Cherbourg on June 27. Collins, the commander of VII Corps, reported: "I witnessed your naval bombardment of the coastal batteries and the covering strongpoints around Cherbourg ... The results were excellent and did much to engage the enemy's fire while our troops stormed into Cherbourg from the rear."[30] Ultimately, the Cherbourg bombardment had neutralized 22 of 24 assigned targets in what the Kriegsmarine's Admiral Krancke reported to be a "naval bombardment of a hitherto unequalled

---

30 *The Invasion of France and Germany* Naval Institute Press (2011)

fierceness." However, little direct destruction of the German batteries was noted; it was the terrifying experience of being shelled that caused German gun crews to quit servicing their guns for long periods. Additionally, guns that could have been turned landwards against Collins' troops had instead been forced to shoot out to sea.

Meanwhile, with *Neptune* operations ending, WNTF responsibilities were phased into a new command under Rear Admiral John Wilkes, called Flag Officer West. Wilkes would successively relieve Moon on June 24, Hall on June 27, and Kirk on July 3. At 0001hrs on July 10, 1944, the Western Naval Task Force was officially dissolved and its USN assets returned to US Twelfth Fleet.

A German Cherbourg battery drops a salvo between the battleships USS *Texas* (background) and USS *Arkansas* (foreground) during the two dreadnoughts' duel with the heavy Battery Hamburg on the afternoon of June 25, 1944. At 32 years old, *Arkansas* was the oldest operational US battleship of World War II, and only two years removed from the US Navy's original dreadnought, USS *Michigan*. (80-G-244210)

ANALYSIS

Although "D-Day" had long been used to refer to the opening day of any major military operation, after *Neptune*, the term would be universally remembered as June 6, 1944. Rear Admiral Kirk would recall: "Courage there was in plenty; but it was the resourcefulness of young sailors, coxswains, junior boat officers, and the skippers and gunnery officers … that made courage and training count."

By D-Day, Rear Admiral Don P. Moon, commander of the highly successful Utah landings, was unknowingly suffering from severe battle fatigue. On August 5, 1944, Moon would commit suicide by shooting himself in the head with his service .45 handgun. One can't help but wonder what may have happened if the psychologically fading Moon – and not the unflinching Hall – had been in command at Omaha.

Naval fire support was one of the most contentious issues at Normandy; pre-invasion and H-Hour fire support plans proved far too rigid and conservative. According to Kirk:

It still seems that our forces are too cautious in the employment of shell fire to support the infantry. There were cases where naval fire was withheld by Army request and in retrospect it is felt that the general attitude was over-cautious. No opportunity should be lost of impressing upon responsible Army officers the dependability and accuracy of naval fire. There were instances in this particular of reports from the beach that our own ships were shelling our own troops on the beach. All of these reports were completely inaccurate, and they had the very unfortunate effect of limiting subsequent fire by captains who no longer trusted their own excellent judgment.[31]

31 *Amphibious Operations. Invasion of Northern France. Western Naval Task Force.* (US Fleet)

However, once the D-Day script was torn up around mid-morning, the resulting improvised naval fire support likely proved decisive at Omaha.

More effective was the post-D-Day naval fire support, which helped seal off the beachhead during its most vulnerable phase. According to Feldmarschall Gerd von Rundstedt, OB West, the commander-in-chief of all German forces in France and the Low Countries: "The fire of your battleships was a main factor in hampering our counterattacks. This was a big surprise." Von Rundstedt's chief-of-staff, General Gunther Blumentritt, agreed, observing that Allied officers interrogating senior German commanders after the war "did not seem to realize the serious effect naval gunfire had on the German defenses."

Even contemporary German military journals praised the Allies' naval gunfire support. According to the *Militaerische Correspondenz Deutschland* of June 16, 1944:

> The fire curtain provided by the guns of the Navy so far proved to be one of the best trump cards of the Anglo-U.S. invasion Armies. It may be that the part played by the Fleet was more decisive than that of the air forces because its fire was better aimed and unlike the bomber formations it had not to confine itself to short "Bursts of Fire."
>
> It would be utterly wrong to underestimate the firepower of warships even of smaller vessels. A Torpedo Boat for instance has the fire power of approximately a Howitzer Battery, a destroyer that of a Battery of Artillery, equivalent to an unusually heavy artillery barrage. Regarding its armament a cruiser may be compared with a Regiment of Artillery. Battleships carrying 38-cm [15in.] or 40-cm [16in.] Guns have a firepower which to achieve in land warfare is difficult and only possible by an unusual concentration of very heavy batteries.
>
> Repeatedly strong formations of warships and cruisers were used against single coastal batteries thus bringing a quite extraordinary superior firepower to bear on them. Moreover time and again he put an umbrella of fire [*Feuerglocke*] over the defenders at the focal points of the fighting compared with which incessant heavy air attacks have only a modest effect.

Interestingly, *Neptune* fire support was light by late-war Pacific standards. For example, between June 6 and June 10 (five days), a total of 1,296 tons of naval projectiles of 3in. caliber and larger were expended against Omaha Beach. This was scarcely one-third what Admiral Raymond Spruance's US Fifth Fleet had used against Kwajalein earlier in 1944, despite Omaha supporting four times as many troops against defensive positions considered three times as strong. As further comparison, Fifth Fleet would later drop 9,907 tons of ordnance on Iwo Jima in the three days leading up to the Detachment Landings, and 3,800 tons of shells and rockets against Okinawa on L-Day (Landing-Day) alone.

SHAEF must be blamed for not more aggressively seeking advice based on Pacific amphibious experience. Indeed, Utah's and Omaha's Major-General

Lawton Collins and Major-General Charles Corlett had both recently been transferred from the Pacific specifically for the Normandy landings. However, unlike SHAEF staff, both Collins and Corlett had experienced fierce Japanese defenses sited directly on the shoreline; neither believed SHAEF was taking their concerns seriously enough. One oft-cited example is SHAEF not using amphibious, tracked LVT ("amtrak") landing craft in the initial Normandy wave, as was standard in the Pacific. LVTs could have ridden directly over the beach to the seawall, providing assault troops with better cover. Indeed, some 300 LVTs had recently been shipped to England, but *Neptune* plans were so far advanced that SHAEF refused to use them.

Nevertheless, considering its scale and scope, the *Neptune* invasion was largely a breathtaking success. Ultimately, a massive amphibious invasion of Northwest Europe played directly to many great American (and British) cultural strengths, such as organization, rationalization, industrial power, and free and open speech – the latter required by officers simply to plan something so massive and dangerous. Consider that on July 4, 1944, the one millionth Allied soldier landed in Normandy, which just four weeks earlier had been the vanguard of Fortress Europe.

Finally, the fact that the Americans assaulted the western Normandy beaches instead of the eastern beaches had profound consequences that are rarely commented upon. Because the Allied armies' ultimate target was Germany, by landing in Normandy the Allies were forced to wheel to the left (east) once they were past the initial Normandy defenses. This sweeping left wheel inevitably put the US Army on the southern flank of the northeast-facing front. However, Allied logistics would largely be supplied from England and through northern French, Belgian, and Dutch ports until the end of the war. This meant the larger and more powerful US Army was on the far side of the Anglo-American line of communications, while the smaller British and Commonwealth forces were closer to the more decisive strategic targets (the Rhine ports, the Ruhr, and Berlin) as well as being in more favorable offensive terrain.

Ultimately, when the shooting stopped in May 1945, it was the British Army that found itself in northwestern Germany, with the US Army deployed in the southwest of the country. When the immediate postwar fallout between the Anglo-Americans and the Soviets led to the Cold War, it meant neither Anglo-American army could leave the Continent; they would instead have to face the Soviet Army and its Warsaw Pact allies across the Inner German Border, right where everyone had halted in May 1945. For the next 45 years, the US Army's large and well-equipped V and VII Corps would be staring down the Warsaw Pact not on the northern flank of West Germany's so-called Central Front, but in the more defensible but arguably less strategically critical south. This was the direct consequence of the Americans landing on Normandy's western beaches on June 6, 1944.

FURTHER READING

Allen, Thomas B., "*The Gallant Destroyers of D-Day*" in Naval History Magazine, Vol. 18, No. 3 (June 2004)

Atkinson, Rick, *The Guns at Last Light: The War in Western Europe, 1944–1945*, Picador, New York (2013)

Bulkley Jr, USNR (Retired), Captain Robert J., *At Close Quarters: PT Boats in the United States Navy*, Naval History Division, Washington (1962)

Center of Military History, CMH Pub 100-12. *Utah Beach to Cherbourg 6 June–27 June 1944*, Center of Military History, US Army, Washington, DC (1990)

Deyo, Vice-Admiral Morton L., *Naval Guns at Normandy,* unpublished

Ford, Ken, *Operation Neptune 1944: D-Day's Seaborne Armada*, Osprey Publishing, Oxford (2014)

Ford, Ken & Zaloga, Steve, *Overlord : The D-Day Landings*, Osprey Publishing, Oxford (2009)

Harrison, Gordon A., CMH Pub 7-4. *The United States Army in World War II. The European Theater of Operations: Cross Channel Attack*, Center of Military History: US Army, Washington, DC (1993)

Johnson, Robert Irwin, *Guardians of the Sea: History of the United States Coast Guard 1915 to the Present*, Naval Institute Press, Annapolis, Maryland (1987)

Kirkland Jr, William B., *Destroyers at Normandy: Naval Gunfire Support at Omaha Beach*, Naval Historical Foundation, Washington, DC (1994)

Morison, Samuel E., *The Invasion of France and Germany 1944–1945*, Naval Institute Press, Annapolis, Maryland (1953)

Padgett, Philip, *Advocating Overlord : The D-Day Strategy and the Atomic Bomb*, Potomac Books, Virginia (2018)

Price, Scott T., *The U.S. Coast Guard at Normandy*, Coast Guard Historian's Office, Washington, DC (1994)

Roskill, Stephen, *The War at Sea, Volume III, Part 2: The Offensive 1 June 1944–14 August 1945*, Naval and Military Press, East Sussex (2004)

Rottman, Gordon L., *D-Day Beach Assault Troops*, Osprey Publishing, Oxford (2017)

Rottman, Gordon L., *US Amphibious Tactics of World War II*, Osprey Publishing, Oxford (2008)

Ruppenthal, Roland G., CMH Pub 7-2-1. *The United States Army in World War II. The European Theater of Operations: Logistical Support of the Armies in Two Volumes. Volume I May 1941–September 1944*, Center of Military History: US Army, Washington, DC (1995)

Symonds, Craig L., *Neptune: The Allied Invasion of Europe and the D-Day Landings*, Oxford University Press, Oxford (2014)

United States Fleet Headquarters of the Commander-in-Chief, *Amphibious Operations. Invasion of Northern France. Western Naval Task Force*, Navy Department, Virginia (June 1944)

U.S. War Department, Historical Division, CMH Pub 100-111. *Omaha Beachhead (6 June–13 June 1944), American Forces in Action series,* War Department (1994)

Exercise Tiger: Disaster at Slapton Sands 28 April 1944, Naval History and Heritage Command

United States Naval Administration in World War II, United States Naval Forces, Europe. Histories. Vol. 5: *Operation NEPTUNE – The Invasion of Normandy* (1948)

Websites

http://usmm.org/normandyships.html

http://www.niehorster.org

https://media.defense.gov/2017/Jul/02/2001772345/-1/-1/0/USCGRESCUEFLOTILLAONEHISTORY.PDF

https://uboat.net

https://ww2talk.com/

https://www.combinedops.org/

https://www.dda*y*-Overlord .com/en/d-day/armada/battle-order/fnfl

https://www.hazegray.org/

https://www.ibiblio.org/hyperwar/

https://www.nationalww2museum.org/war/articles/*uss*-Texas-battery-hamburg-1944

https://www.navsource.org

http://www.navweaps.com/

https://www.navymemorial.org/tales-from-the-navy-log/2020/6/4/catching-heat-in-new-york-and-normandy-yogi-berra-at-d-day

INDEX